Better Homes and Gardens® Books
An imprint of Meredith® Books

EatingForLife

Editor: Kristi M.Fuller, R.D.
Contributing Editors: Catherine Cogliandro Alioto, Marlene Brown,
Ken Haedrich, Connie Hay, Laura J. Pensiero
Contributing Writers: Susan Pittman, Diane Quagliani, R.D., Marcia Stanley, R.D.
Senior Associate Art Director: Ken Carlson
Copy Chief: Terri Fredrickson
Managers, Book Production: Pam Kvitne, Marjorie J. Schenkelberg
Contributing Copy Editor: Daniel Cubias
Contributing Proofreaders: Pegi Bevins, Maria Duryee, Gretchen Kauffman
Photographers: Pete Krumhardt, Joyce Oedkerk Pool
Food Stylists: Charles Worthington, Dianna Nolin
Prop Stylist: Karen Johnson
Indexer: Martha Fifield
Electronic Production Coordinator: Paula Forest
Editorial and Design Assistants: Judy Bailey, Mary Lee Gavin, Karen Schirm
Test Kitchen Director: Lynn Blanchard
Test Kitchen Product Supervisor: Marilyn Cornelius

Meredith® Books

Editor in Chief: James D. Blume
Design Director: Matt Strelecki
Managing Editor: Gregory H. Kayko
Executive Food Editor: Jennifer Dorland Darling

Director, Retail Sales and Marketing: Terry Unsworth
Director, Sales, Special Markets: Rita McMullen
Director, Sales, Premiums: Michael A. Peterson
Director, Sales, Retail: Tom Wierzbicki
Director, Book Marketing: Brad Elmitt
Director, Operations: George A. Susral
Director, Production: Douglas M. Johnston

Vice President, General Manager: Jamie L. Martin

Better Homes and Gardens® Magazine

Editor in Chief: Jean LemMon
Executive Food Editor: Nancy Byal

Meredith Publishing Group

President, Publishing Group: Stephen M. Lacy
Vice President, Finance and Administration: Max Runciman

Meredith Corporation

Chairman and Chief Executive Officer: William T. Kerr

Chairman of the Executive Committee: E. T. Meredith III

Our seal assures you that every recipe in _Eating For Life_ has been tested in the
Better Homes and Gardens® Test Kitchen. This means that each recipe is practical and reliable, and meets our
high standards of taste appeal. We guarantee your satisfaction with this book for as long as you own it.

Better Homes and Gardens®

EatingForLife

Boost Immunity • Prevent Disease • Celebrate Good Food

Better Homes and Gardens® Books
Des Moines, Iowa

Grilled Greek-Style Turkey Burgers, page 113

Contents

ToLife!

Once upon a time, you may have been told to eat your vegetables. The reasoning may have been "Because they're good for you." Today, research shows that eating your vegetables (and certain fruits, lean meats, and fish) can actually reduce your risk for various diseases, such as cancer or heart disease, and can promote good health.

These miraculous health-promoting foods have become known as functional foods (learn more about specific foods to include in your diet, pages 8 to 21). As clinical as that term might sound, it doesn't have to take on scary connotations and conjure memories of tasteless foods. One of the most pleasurable things in life is enjoying good food. Gone are the days that require you to deprive yourself of the foods you love in order to stay healthy. You can have satisfying meals—and eat healthfully. *Eating For Life* exemplifies the pleasurable aspects of food and eating well.

To use this book, you'll find a chart with each recipe which highlights the positive aspects of the recipe. Worried about osteoporosis? You'll know at a glance which recipe zeros in on that particular health issue. The charts provide a quick way to see how foods you eat can positively impact your health. Isn't that why you want to eat better? Being healthy allows you to spend more time doing things you most enjoy. As more research becomes available, it's clear that what you eat can help you live longer and healthier. Get ready to celebrate a long, healthy life with 115 tasty recipes from which to choose!

Mediterranean Chicken and Pasta, page 103

MiracleFoods

Gastronomy: The Art or Science of Good Eating

Ten of your closest friends arrive for a fabulous feast. The evening begins with a selection of crudités and whole wheat crackers with Carrot Hummus (recipe, page 183). Red grapes, a selection of cheeses, and a variety of nuts adorn the center of the table. The main course, succulent Pepper Steak with Horseradish Sauce (recipe, page 62), is accompanied by a sauteed medley of asparagus, corn, baby carrots, peas, and broccoli. For your vegetarian friends, you've prepared Fried Tofu and Watercress Salad (recipe, page 138) with a ginger vinaigrette. For dessert you serve Pineapple-Pear Crisp (recipe, page 177) with a hazelnut-oat topping along with your favorite green tea.

Your culinary dexterity will no doubt wow your friends. However, what you (and they) may not know is that the meal you prepared has an additional dimension chock-full of healthful components. From the horseradish on the beef to the medley of vegetables to the after-dinner tea with dessert, the ingredients that make up this gastronomic treat pack health-promoting potential into your day. That's great news to anyone who is concerned about health. The more you know about the science of food, the easier it is to choose foods that are best for you and your family.

Functional Foods and Disease Prevention

What we eat plays an important role in preventing many diseases, including heart disease, cancer, and osteoporosis. Eating a balanced diet with a variety of foods and maintaining an active lifestyle are two keys to promoting health and well-being. Some foods, however, provide health benefits beyond basic nutrition. These foods are termed "functional foods."

Functional foods do more than meet your minimum daily requirements of nutrients. They also can play roles in reducing the risk of disease and promoting good health. Basic nutrition

concentrates on foods and nutrients needed for normal growth and development. Vitamins, minerals, carbohydrates, proteins, and fats are some of the basic nutrients that the body needs. While all foods are functional in that they provide nutrients, the term "functional foods" describes health-promoting ingredients or natural components that have a potential benefit to the body. This includes whole foods as well as fortified, enriched, or enhanced foods and dietary supplements.

History of Functional Foods

The concept of functional foods is not new, although dramatic advances have been made recently. In the early 1900s, food manufacturers in the United States began adding iodine to salt to prevent goiters (an enlargement of the thyroid gland), representing one of the first attempts at creating a functional component through fortification.

Today, researchers have identified hundreds of compounds with functional qualities, and they continue to make new discoveries about the complex benefits of phytochemicals (plant chemicals) in foods. Phytochemicals are found in many foods and can provide benefits beyond basic nutrition. Many functional foods have these chemicals present.

All foods are beneficial in one way or another. They provide taste, texture, aroma, and nutritional value, which is why it's important to include choices from all the food groups in well-rounded meals. However, a food is functional in different ways. Research and education have changed or even improved our perception of the qualities of natural whole foods. Modern science has also actually changed characteristics of many foods via plant breeding and manu-facturing processes.

Research has shown that many—if not most—fruits, vegetables, grains, fish, and dairy and meat products contain several natural components that deliver benefits beyond basic nutrition, such as lycopene in tomatoes, omega-3 fatty acids in salmon, and saponins in soybeans. Some studies have noted that even certain types of tea and chocolate have bene-ficial health attributes.

Agricultural scientists can boost the nutritional content of certain food crops—everything from beta-carotene-rich rice to vitamin-enhanced broccoli and soybeans—through the same breeding techniques used to strengthen desirable traits in plants and animals Research is under way to improve the nutritional quality of dozens of other food crops.

Other foods get a boost during processing with added nutrients or other ingredients. This is true of products such as orange juice fortified with calcium, cereals with added vitamins or minerals, and flour with added folic acid. In fact, more foods are being fortified with nutrients and other physiologically active components as researchers uncover evidence about the components' role in health and disease-risk reduction.

The scientific community has just begun to understand the complex interactions between nutritional components and the human body. However, there is already a large body of scientific evidence that shows eating functional foods on a regular basis as part of a varied diet can help reduce the risk or decrease the severity of many health concerns, including cancer, heart and cardiovascular disease, gastroin-testinal ailments, menopausal symptoms, osteoporosis, and eye problems due to aging.

As our knowledge increases, so does our interest in eating functional foods for the potential health benefits. Look at functional foods and determine which ones, if included in your culinary and wellness plan, can help keep you healthy.

Soy Good

Soy is good food. It is well worth adding to your diet—as tofu, edamame (soybeans), soy milk, soy flour, tempeh, and textured soy protein, to name a few sources. Eating soy daily

can lower blood cholesterol levels. Food with moderate to high levels of soy protein can now don an official health label linking it to heart health. Soy is associated with several other potential health benefits including a reduced risk of cancer and the maintenance or improvement of bone health. It is uncertain if the beneficial substance in soy is the protein itself or the numerous plant estrogens called isoflavones. Isoflavones are a type of phytoestrogen, plant substances that seem to act as antioxidants and mild estrogens.

Soy, in its many forms, is a healthful ingredient for all to enjoy, but it's especially good for vegetarians. Besides its potential health benefits, soy is a great source of protein, which can sometimes be lacking in strict vegetarian diets. However, because no food is a magic bullet, it is still important to eat soy as part of a varied diet.

You Say Tomato

Another food to take advantage of is the not-so-humble tomato. Tomatoes offer vitamin C and a lot more. They are rich in important carotenoids, including lycopene, a relative of the famed beta-carotene. Whole tomatoes and tomato products, including tomato sauce, tomato paste, pizza sauce, tomato juice, and tomato-based soups and stews, all contain lycopene, which may help reduce the risk of prostate cancer.

What's interesting about this recently discovered carotenoid is that it seems the body can better absorb it from tomatoes that are cooked and processed. Ounce for ounce, cooked and processed tomatoes and tomato products contain up to 10 times more lycopene than fresh tomatoes do.

Perhaps the best news of all is that because lycopene is a fat-soluble compound, it is better absorbed if it is eaten or cooked with a small amount of fat. So go ahead and prepare your pasta sauce with a little olive oil and leave out the guilt.

Nuttin' But Good News

Take heart if you love nuts and can't give them up. Nuts have always been valued for their protein, vitamins, and minerals. But they have hidden talents as well. Recent studies show that nuts help reduce the risk of heart disease. They are rich in fats, but those fats are mostly unsaturated fats, including monounsaturated fats—the same kinds that gave olive oil its good name. Nuts are also a great source of vitamin E, fiber, folic acid, and other B vitamins. The best way to enjoy the health benefits of nuts is to choose unsalted varieties and eat only small amounts. Add them to salads, rice dishes, cereals, cakes, and muffins.

That Stinkin' Rose (The Garlic Family)

Garlic dates back to ancient Egypt, Greece, and Rome as a treatment for disease and a stabilizer of health. It was also thought to enhance performance and, as such, was given to Olympic athletes in Greece prior to competitions. In biblical times, garlic was used as currency. In ancient China and Japan, it was used as a food preservative. Interest in the benefits of garlic has not diminished over thousands of years. Modern research is confirming many beliefs of ancient medicine.

Despite this golden history, garlic is often maligned as a cause of strong odor on the breath after consuming. But garlic's benefits far outweigh this problem. The garlic family, including onion-family members such as leeks, chives, shallots, and scallions, contains allylic sulfides and other compounds that may reduce the risk of cancerous tumors. Benefits to the heart are also noted characteristics of garlic. Furthermore, eating garlic can help control blood pressure. Garlic also has been shown to effectively suppress harmful effects of low-density-lipoprotein (LDL or "bad") cholesterol.

Although garlic has been studied extensively for decades, not all of its active components are known. Additional research is needed to identify more of garlic's health benefits

and determine how specific compounds in garlic interact with each other and with other foods. It is believed that some of garlic's numerous compounds transform into other substances, some of which have protective effects. Eating as little as a clove of garlic a day may be beneficial. It also appears that the way garlic and onions are prepared plays a role in their effectiveness against disease. When raw garlic is crushed or chopped, its compounds convert into the active protective form. So when making a recipe that calls for fresh garlic, chop the garlic first and let it stand for at least 10 minutes while you prepare the other ingredients. This allows the active protectors to form before cooking halts the conversion process. Better yet, eat fresh garlic whenever possible, because it might be more potent than heated garlic.

Facts About Fish

One of the most exciting facts about fish, when it comes to nutrition, regards omega-3 fatty acids. Fatty fish from cold-water regions, such as tuna, salmon, mackerel, and sardines, contain this kind of fat. These healthful fats reduce the risk of heart disease.

Yes, fats can do that. The three major categories of dietary fats—saturated, monounsaturated, and polyunsaturated—have effects on less desirable LDL cholesterol and the more desirable high-density-lipoprotein (HDL) cholesterol levels. Saturated fats, in general, have been shown to elevate LDL cholesterol levels, and high levels of LDL cholesterol are a major risk factor for heart disease. In contrast, diets high in monounsaturated and polyunsaturated fats lower LDL cholesterol levels. The polyunsaturated fat category contains two subclasses of fatty acids: omega-6 (n-6) fatty acids and omega-3 (n-3) fatty acids. Vegetable oils, such as corn, sunflower, safflower, and soybean, are rich in n-6 fatty acids. Besides fatty fish, soybean oil is an excellent source of n-3 fatty acids, as are canola oil and deep-sea fish.

The American Heart Association recommends eating at least two servings (3 ounces each) of fish weekly to help reduce the risk of heart disease.

Oh, Those Oats and Other Grains

A few years ago, one convincing study about oats created a plethora of oat-based products. The obsession with oats quelled for a time, but oats are back in vogue. The first food-based health claim that the Food and Drug Administration (FDA) approved was for oats. Oats, oat bran, and whole-oat products contain the soluble fiber beta-glucan, which aids in decreasing blood cholesterol levels by binding bile acids in the intestine. This process helps to carry cholesterol out of the body.

The FDA's health claim for oats was a decreased risk of cardiovascular disease. The FDA stated that foods containing whole oats (whole oats, oat bran, and oat flour) must have at least .75 grams of soluble fiber per serving to benefit the heart. (This type of fiber is soluble in water and acts like a sponge in the body, soaking up toxins.) This translates to 1½ cups of cooked oatmeal, 1 cup of cooked oat-bran cereal, or 3 cups of ready-to-eat cereal with oats. Eating oats as part of a balanced breakfast with oatmeal, fat-free or soy milk, fruit, and juice is a quick and healthful way to start your day.

Psyllium, another soluble fiber, has health effects similar to beta-glucan. It's found in dried beans, peas, barley, apples, citrus fruits, corn, flaxseed, and, also, oats and oat bran. The benefits of psyllium don't stop with heart disease. Whole-grain foods can also reduce the risk of breast and colon cancers. Brown rice, oatmeal, corn bran, wheat germ, and breads (those listing whole wheat as the first ingredient) are good sources of whole grains, which contain insoluble fiber. (Insoluble fiber is not soluble in water and acts like a broom in the body, sweeping away waste.) Refined grains, used in white bread or white flour, have almost all phytochemicals removed. Therefore, choose whole-grain foods when you can.

The Deeper the Color, the Better

Deeply colored fruits and vegetables tend to have the most vitamins and minerals. Also, the pigments that give these fruits and vegetables their rich colors might protect against some diseases. These pigments have high antioxidant potential. Antioxidants are compounds that help to stabilize free radicals in the body. This helps to reduce the risk of developing chronic diseases such as cancer because the antioxidant keeps the free radical from damaging cells in the body. This doesn't mean that you should ignore iceberg lettuce, cauliflower, white potatoes, and turnips. They too play an important role in culinary pleasures. However, stock up regularly on richly colored foods such as kale, spinach, collard greens, cranberries, raisins, dried plums (prunes), red grapes, carrots, and cherries.

Tea for Two

Most teas—green, black, red, and oolong (though not herb teas)—contain a potpourri of potentially beneficial phytochemicals that may reduce the risk of many cancers, such as stomach, throat, and skin cancers. Tea, the second most-consumed beverage in the world, has an abundance of flavonoids called catechins, which are a type of antioxidant. Drinking tea regularly can also protect arteries from plaque buildup. Green tea contains higher amounts of catechins than do black and red teas because it is fermented less. Brewing methods, such as steeping longer, may increase the antioxidant level in the tea.

Red, Red Wine (and Purple Grape Juice)

The purple grapes used to make red wine and purple grape juice contain types of phytochemicals called polyphenolic compounds. These compounds support normal, healthy heart functioning. The polyphenolic compound found in the skin and seeds of grapes (used in making purple grape juice and red wine) has a special anticlotting function, which reduces plaque buildup in the arteries. This substance also helps to keep LDL ("bad") cholesterol from attaching to the arteries. Therefore, including purple grape juice in your fruit consumption, a few times a week, has an added health bonus. These compounds are also found in many other fruits, including cranberries, blueberries, and raspberries. Despite the benefits of red wine, it is not recommended that you begin drinking wine or other alcoholic beverages if you do not already do so. If you consume wine, it is recommended that you do so in moderation.

The Best for Last: Chocolate

It's true—chocolate is good for you! Chocolate contains large amounts of catechins, the same beneficial compounds found in tea. Chocolate has the same beneficial effect as tea, and it seems to pack a lot of antioxidants per ounce. Just 1 ounce of chocolate has about as much beneficial catechin as 1 cup of brewed black tea. If you like dark chocolate, the news is even better. The darker the chocolate, the higher it's likely to be in flavonoids. However, as with many of the beneficial compounds being discovered in foods, it is unclear how much chocolate you need to eat to achieve benefits. So until more research is done, save chocolate for an occasional treat because it's high in calories, fat, and sugar, and low in fiber.

How to Get More Functional Foods into Your Diet

While the benefits of any food depend on a person's overall diet, the evidence that foods provide specific health benefits and reduce the risk of certain diseases will not likely be refuted soon. The most effective way to reap the many health benefits from foods is to eat a balanced and varied diet, emphasizing fruits, vegetables, and foods with added beneficial components.

Before you make any major dietary changes, however, evaluate your personal health or speak to your doctor about ways to reduce your risk of certain diseases. It is important to remember that there is no single magic food that can cure or prevent most health concerns. The best advice is to

choose foods wisely from each level of the food pyramid to incorporate many potentially beneficial components into your diet (see chart *below* for listing of chemical compound names, food sources, and potential health benefits).

Since 1993, the FDA has approved 13 health claims, eight of which are related to the functional benefits of food:

- Fruits and vegetables relating to cancer
- Plant sterol and plant stanol relating to coronary heart disease
- Soy protein relating to coronary heart disease
- Calcium relating to the reduced risk of osteoporosis
- Fiber-containing grain products, fruits, and vegetables relating to cancer (continued on page 21)

Phytochemical	Sources	Potential Health Benefit
Allylic sulfides	Garlic, chives, leeks, onions, shallots	Detoxifies; offers cancer resistance; antiviral properties
Beta-carotene	Apricots, carrots, squash, peaches	Enhances immunity; helps prevent cataracts; slows cancer progression
Catechins	Green and black teas, chocolate	Prevents cancer
Diadzein	Soybeans, tofu	Prevents estrogen from binding to receptors; has anticancer potential
Ellagic acid	Blackberries, cranberries, grapes, strawberries, walnuts	Provides antioxidants
Genestein	Tofu, soy milk, soy beans	Inhibits tumor growth; protects against heart disease
Isothiocyanates	Cruciferous vegetables (broccoli, kale, cabbage, cauliflower)	Reduces risk of cancer
Lutein	Spinach, collard greens, kale	Protects against age-related eye disease; decreases risk for lung disease
Lycopene	Tomatoes, kiwifruit	Reduces risk of prostate cancer
Monoterpenes	Orange and citrus oils, kale	Slows growth of cancer cells
Omega-3 fatty acids	Fish oil (mackerel, salmon, trout)	Reduces risk of heart disease
Proanthocyanidins	Cranberries, cranberry products, cocoa, chocolate	Improves urinary tract health; reduces risk of cardiovascular disease
Resveratrol	Grapes, red wine, peanuts	Lowers blood pressure and risk of heart disease
Saponins	Soybeans, soy foods	Helps to lower LDL cholesterol, controls blood sugars, and prevents cancer
Zeaxanthin	Arugula, collards, horseradish, yellow corn, mustard, sorrel	Provides antioxidants; boosts immune function

Note: This table is not all encompassing. Researchers continue to identify potentially beneficial components in food at a rapid rate.

- Potassium relating to the reduced risk of high blood pressure and stroke
- Fruits, vegetables, and grain products that contain fiber, particularly soluble fiber, relating to the risk of coronary heart disease
- Folate relating to neural-tube birth defects
- Dietary soluble fiber, such as that found in whole oats and psyllium seed husk, relating to coronary heart disease
- Dietary sugar alcohol relating to dental cavities

The remaining three claims are based on negative health impacts of certain nutrients in food:
- Dietary fat relating to cancer
- Dietary saturated fat relating to cholesterol and risk of coronary heart disease
- Sodium relating to high blood pressure.

Glossary

Antioxidants The most important benefit of vitamins A, E, C and many carotenoids and phytochemicals is their role as antioxidants. Antioxidants are scavengers of free radicals. The unstable particles are the by-products of normal body processes and are increased by smoking, environmental toxins, and stress. These particles can damage cell membranes and contribute to diseases such as cancer, heart disease, cataracts, and even aging. Antioxidants neutralize free radicals and help prevent cell damage.

Carcinogens Any substance or agent that produces or causes cancer.

Conjugated Linoleic Acid (CLA) A potent, naturally occurring anticarcinogen found exclusively in animal products. CLA, a fatty acid found mainly in milk fat and dairy products, is abundant in the meat of cows and sheep. Cooking the meat increases the amount of CLA. Fat-free or low-fat dairy foods contain little CLA.

Cruciferous vegetables Plants from the cabbage family such as broccoli, cauliflower, cabbage, Brussels sprouts, and kohlrabi. These vegetables contain sulforaphane and isothiocynates that appear to help stimulate the production of anticancer enzymes in the body. Indoles, which are also found in these particular foods, also help reduce breast cancer risk. Indoles are not destroyed by cooking and might actually increase in number during cooking.

Free radicals Unstable molecules resulting from normal metabolic processes. During these processes, oxygen molecules lose an electron, which creates an unstable molecule (free radical), thereby causing oxidative stress. These free radicals attack healthy cells in the body in the hopes of finding another electron to stabilize themselves. This process can damage healthy cells.

Functional food components Nutritive and nonnutritive compounds that are thought to reduce the risk of disease or promote health.

Functional foods Foods that provide a health benefit beyond basic nutrition.

Health claim A scientific-based health claim allowed on food labels by the Food and Drug Administration. A claim must have sufficient scientific agreement among qualified health experts that it is factual. The claim indicates a relationship between a nutrient or other food substance and a disease or health-related condition.

Phytochemicals Naturally occurring constituents of plant foods that are currently under scientific investigation to determine their potential benefits for reducing the risk of health problems, including cancer, cardiovascular disease, rheumatoid arthritis, hypertension, and others.

Phytoestrogens A group of naturally occurring chemicals derived from plants. They have a structure similar to estrogen and block estrogen receptor sites on cells. This helps prevent potentially anticarcinogenic activity in the body.

Breakfast Brunch

Blueberry Blintzes, page 24

Blueberry Blintzes   **Prep:** 30 minutes **Bake:** 15 minutes

Showcase naturally sweet and juicy summer blueberries in this spectacular brunch entrée. The blueberries provide high levels of antioxidants to fight cancer and to slow aging. Rich ricotta cheese filling adds calcium for heart protection. (Pictured on page 23.)

2 eggs	$^1/_4$ cup packed brown sugar
$1^1/_3$ cups fat-free milk	$1^1/_2$ teaspoons finely shredded orange peel
$^3/_4$ cup whole wheat flour	1 cup orange juice
1 tablespoon cooking oil	1 tablespoon cornstarch
$^1/_4$ teaspoon salt	1 tablespoon granulated sugar
1 15-ounce carton part-skim ricotta cheese	$^1/_4$ teaspoon ground cardamom
2 cups blueberries	

1 For crepes, in a medium bowl combine eggs, milk, flour, oil, and salt; beat until well mixed. Heat a lightly greased 6-inch skillet over medium heat; remove from heat. Spoon in 2 tablespoons batter; lift and tilt skillet to spread batter. Return to heat; cook on one side only for 1 to 2 minutes or until brown. Invert over clean, white paper towels; remove crepe. Repeat with the remaining batter, lightly greasing skillet occasionally.

2 For filling, in another medium bowl combine ricotta cheese, 1 cup of the blueberries, the brown sugar, and 1 teaspoon of the orange peel. Fill each crepe, browned side down, with a rounded tablespoon of the filling. Roll up. Place blintzes in a 3-quart rectangular baking dish. Bake, uncovered, in a 400° oven for 15 to 20 minutes or until heated through.

3 Meanwhile, for sauce, in a small saucepan stir together the remaining $^1/_2$ teaspoon orange peel, the orange juice, cornstarch, granulated sugar, and cardamom. Cook and stir until thickened and bubbly. Cook and stir for 2 minutes more. Stir in the remaining 1 cup blueberries. Spoon sauce over warm blintzes. Makes 8 servings (16 blintzes).

Nutrition Facts per serving: 229 cal., 8 g total fat (3 g sat. fat), 70 mg chol., 181 mg sodium, 31 g carbo., 2 g fiber, 11 g pro.
Daily Values: 10% vit. A, 35% vit. C, 22% calcium, 7% iron
Exchanges: $1^1/_2$ Fruit, $^1/_2$ Starch, $1^1/_2$ Lean Meat, $^1/_2$ Fat

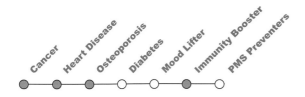

Tofu And Veggie Breakfast Burritos   **Start to Finish:** 35 minutes

These spicy burritos feature protein-rich tofu. This mild-tasting soy food takes on the flavors of what it's paired with. Researchers are investigating whether phytoestrogens in soy foods help reduce bone loss in postmenopausal women. To promote healthy bones, choose a tofu that contains calcium.

2 tiny new potatoes, cut into $^1\!/_2$-inch cubes	1 12- to 16-ounce package extra-firm tofu (fresh bean curd), cut into $^1\!/_2$-inch cubes
1 medium zucchini, cut into thin bite-size strips	$^1\!/_2$ cup water
1 medium red sweet pepper, thinly sliced	3 tablespoons tamari sauce or reduced-sodium soy sauce
$^1\!/_2$ cup finely chopped onion	2 teaspoons curry powder
3 cloves garlic, minced	1 vegetable or chicken bouillon cube
1 tablespoon olive oil	8 8- to 10-inch spinach flour tortillas

1 In a medium covered saucepan cook potatoes in a small amount of boiling, lightly salted water for 10 to 12 minutes or until tender; drain.

2 Meanwhile, for filling, in a large nonstick skillet cook zucchini, sweet pepper, onion, and garlic in hot oil over medium heat about 5 minutes or until vegetables are tender. Stir in potatoes, tofu, water, tamari sauce, curry powder, and bouillon cube. Cook about 10 minutes more or until most of the liquid is evaporated, stirring occasionally.

3 Wrap tortillas in microwave-safe paper towels. Microwave on 100% power (high) for 30 to 60 seconds or until tortillas are warm.

4 To serve, spoon filling down center of tortillas. Fold one end to partially cover filling; roll up from an adjacent side. Serve immediately. Makes 8 servings.*

Nutrition Facts per serving: 291 cal., 6 g total fat (0 g sat. fat), 2 mg chol., 1,133 mg sodium, 47 g carbo., 2 g fiber, 12 g pro.
Daily Values: 16% vit. A, 48% vit. C, 7% calcium, 18% iron
Exchanges: 3 Starch, 1 Medium Fat Meat

---

*Note: If you need only 4 burritos for breakfast, cover and refrigerate half of the filling for up to 2 days. To serve, transfer filling to a microwave-safe container; cover with waxed paper. Microwave on 100% power (high) for $2^1\!/_2$ to $3^1\!/_2$ minutes or until heated through, stirring once. Heat and fill tortillas as above.

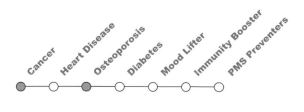

Cancer Heart Disease Osteoporosis Diabetes Mood Lifter Immunity Booster PMS Preventers

Wheat Germ Carrot Muffins

Prep: 15 minutes   **Bake:** 20 minutes

Wake up to one of these antioxidant-rich muffins. Wheat germ is a terrific source of vitamin E, and carrots, of course, are loaded with carotenoids. Studies show that raisins exhibit high-power antioxidant activity.

Nonstick cooking spray	½ teaspoon ground cinnamon
1 cup golden raisins or dried currants	1 beaten egg
2 cups all-purpose flour	1¼ cups buttermilk
⅓ cup toasted wheat germ	½ cup packed brown sugar
1½ teaspoons baking powder	¼ cup cooking oil
½ teaspoon baking soda	1 cup shredded carrot
½ teaspoon salt	

1 Lightly coat twelve 2½-inch muffin cups with cooking spray; set aside. In a small bowl pour enough boiling water over raisins to cover; set aside.

2 In a medium bowl combine the flour, wheat germ, baking powder, baking soda, salt, and cinnamon. Make a well in the center of flour mixture.

3 In a small bowl combine the egg, buttermilk, brown sugar, and oil. Add the egg mixture all at once to flour mixture. Stir just until moistened (batter should be lumpy). Drain raisins. Gently fold raisins and carrot into batter.

4 Spoon batter into the prepared muffin cups, filling each about three-fourths full. Bake in a 400° oven about 20 minutes or until golden brown. Cool in pan on a wire rack for 5 minutes. Remove from muffin cups. Serve warm. Makes 12 muffins.

Nutrition Facts per muffin: 226 cal., 6 g total fat (1 g sat. fat), 19 mg chol., 242 mg sodium, 39 g carbo., 2 g fiber, 5 g pro.
Daily Values: 52% vit. A, 3% vit. C, 9% calcium, 11% iron
Exchanges: ½ Fruit, 2 Starch, 1 Fat

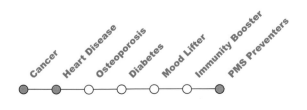

Chunky Apple-Pumpkin Muffins   **Prep:** 20 minutes **Bake:** 20 minutes

Pumpkin is for more than just the holidays. It's a great source of beta-carotene, which enhances immunity and offers protection against cancer and heart disease. The apples spiking these spicy muffins lend soluble fiber to control blood sugars and lower cholesterol.

Nonstick cooking spray	¹/₂ cup applesauce
1 cup all-purpose flour	¹/₂ cup refrigerated or frozen egg product, thawed
²/₃ cup whole wheat flour	¹/₃ cup packed brown sugar
1¹/₂ teaspoons baking powder	¹/₄ cup fat-free milk
1 teaspoon pumpkin pie spice	2 tablespoons cooking oil
¹/₂ teaspoon salt	¹/₂ cup finely chopped cooking apple
³/₄ cup canned pumpkin	¹/₂ cup salted pumpkin seeds, toasted

1 Lightly coat twelve 2¹/₂-inch muffin cups with cooking spray; set aside. In a large bowl combine the all-purpose flour, whole wheat flour, baking powder, pumpkin pie spice, and salt. Make a well in the center of flour mixture.

2 In a medium bowl combine the pumpkin, applesauce, egg product, brown sugar, milk, and oil. Add the egg mixture all at once to flour mixture. Stir just until moistened (batter should be lumpy). Gently fold in apple and pumpkin seeds.

3 Spoon batter into the prepared muffin cups, filling each about three-fourths full. Bake in a 375° oven for 20 to 25 minutes or until golden brown. Cool in pan on a wire rack for 5 minutes. Remove from muffin cups. Serve warm. Makes 12 muffins.

Nutrition Facts per muffin: 176 cal., 7 g total fat (1 g sat. fat), 0 mg chol., 225 mg sodium, 24 g carbo., 2 g fiber, 6 g pro.
Daily Values: 69% vit. A, 2% vit. C, 6% calcium, 15% iron
Exchanges: 1¹/₂ Starch, 1 Fat

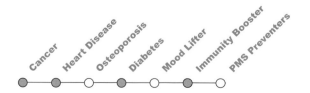

Pumpkin Pancakes With Orange Syrup

Start to Finish: 30 minutes

This antioxidant-loaded dish is perfect brunch fare. The pumpkin in the pancakes provides carotenoids and phenolic compounds; the orange juice in the syrup adds vitamin C.

2	cups all-purpose flour	1	cup canned pumpkin
2	tablespoons brown sugar	1/2	cup refrigerated or frozen egg product, thawed
1	tablespoon baking powder	2	tablespoons cooking oil
1/2	teaspoon salt		Nonstick cooking spray
1/2	teaspoon pumpkin pie spice	1	recipe Orange Syrup
1 1/2	cups fat-free milk	1	orange, peeled and sectioned (optional)

1 In a medium bowl stir together the flour, brown sugar, baking powder, salt, and pumpkin pie spice. Make a well in the center of the flour mixture.

2 In another medium bowl combine the milk, pumpkin, egg product, and oil. Add the milk mixture all at once to flour mixture. Stir just until moistened (batter should be lumpy).

3 Lightly coat a nonstick griddle or heavy skillet with cooking spray. Heat over medium heat. For each pancake, pour about 1/4 cup batter onto the hot griddle or skillet. Cook over medium heat about 2 minutes or until pancakes have bubbly surfaces and edges are slightly dry. Turn pancakes; cook about 2 minutes more or until golden brown. Serve warm with Orange Syrup and, if desired, orange sections. Makes 16 pancakes.

Orange Syrup: In a small saucepan stir together 1 cup orange juice, 2 tablespoons honey, 2 1/2 teaspoons cornstarch, and 1/4 teaspoon ground cinnamon. Cook and stir until thickened and bubbly. Cook and stir for 2 minutes more. Serve warm. Makes about 1 cup.

Nutrition Facts per pancake: 110 cal., 2 g total fat (0 g sat. fat), 0 mg chol., 174 mg sodium, 20 g carbo., 1 g fiber, 3 g pro.
Daily Values: 70% vit. A, 15% vit. C, 9% calcium, 7% iron
Exchanges: 1/2 Fruit, 1 Starch

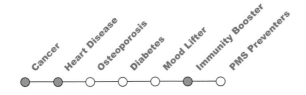

Cancer · Heart Disease · Osteoporosis · Diabetes · Mood Lifter · Immunity Booster · PMS Preventers

Macadamia Pancakes With Dried Fruit

Start to Finish: 30 minutes

The macadamia nuts in these island-inspired pancakes are rich in monounsaturated fat, which can help lower blood cholesterol levels. Like other nuts, macadamias contain vitamin E, an antioxidant that helps fight heart disease.

½ cup buckwheat flour	¼ cup refrigerated or frozen egg product, thawed
½ cup whole wheat flour	2 tablespoons cooking oil
1 tablespoon brown sugar	¼ cup chopped macadamia nuts
2 teaspoons baking powder	¼ cup tropical blend mixed dried fruit bits
¼ teaspoon salt	Nonstick cooking spray
1 cup fat-free milk	1 recipe Quick Tropical Yogurt Sauce

1 In a medium bowl stir together buckwheat flour, whole wheat flour, brown sugar, baking powder, and salt. Make a well in the center of flour mixture.

2 In another medium bowl combine milk, egg product, and oil. Add the egg mixture all at once to flour mixture. Stir just until moistened (batter should be lumpy). Gently fold in nuts and dried fruit bits.

3 Lightly coat a nonstick griddle or heavy skillet with cooking spray. Heat over medium heat. For each pancake, pour about ¼ cup batter onto hot griddle or skillet. Spread batter into a circle about 4 inches in diameter. Cook over medium heat for 2 minutes or until pancakes have bubbly surfaces and edges are slightly dry. Turn pancakes; cook for 2 minutes more or until browned. Serve warm with Quick Tropical Yogurt Sauce. Makes 8 pancakes.

Quick Tropical Yogurt Sauce: In a small bowl stir together one 8-ounce carton piña colada or vanilla low-fat yogurt and ¼ cup tropical blend mixed dried fruit bits. Makes about 1 cup.

Nutrition Facts per pancake: 352 cal., 15 g total fat (3 g sat. fat), 4 mg chol., 454 mg sodium, 48 g carbo., 4 g fiber, 12 g pro.
Daily Values: 4% vit. A, 3% vit. C, 33% calcium, 12% iron
Exchanges: ½ Milk, ½ Fruit, 1 Starch, 1 Fat

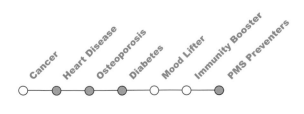

Three-Grain Flapjacks

Start to Finish: 30 minutes

For a tasty fiber and phytochemical boost, top these wholesome flapjacks with fresh fruit. If your favorite isn't in season, choose frozen, canned, or jarred fruits, which are processed at the peak of freshness and offer the same health benefits as fresh fruit.

1½	cups all-purpose flour	1¾	cups light milk
½	cup yellow cornmeal	¼	cup plain low-fat yogurt
2½	teaspoons baking powder	3	tablespoons cooking oil
½	teaspoon salt	½	cup dried blueberries or currants (optional)
½	cup regular rolled oats		Nonstick cooking spray
3	tablespoons brown sugar		Maple syrup or reduced-calorie maple-flavored syrup (optional)
1	beaten egg		

1 In a large bowl stir together flour, cornmeal, baking powder, and salt. In a blender container or food processor bowl combine oats and brown sugar. Cover and blend or process until oats are coarsely ground. Stir oat mixture into flour mixture. Make a well in the center of flour mixture.

2 In a medium bowl combine the egg, milk, yogurt, and oil. Add the egg mixture all at once to flour mixture. Stir just until moistened (batter should be lumpy and thin). Let stand for 10 minutes to thicken slightly, stirring once or twice. If desired, gently fold in blueberries.

3 Lightly coat a nonstick griddle or heavy skillet with cooking spray. Heat over medium heat. For each pancake, pour about ¼ cup batter onto the hot griddle or skillet. Cook over medium heat for 1½ to 2 minutes or until pancakes have bubbly surfaces and the edges are slightly dry. Turn pancakes; cook for 1½ to 2 minutes more or until golden brown. If desired, serve with syrup. Makes 16 to 20 pancakes.

Nutrition Facts per pancake: 117 cal., 4 g total fat (2 g sat. fat), 31 mg chol., 312 mg sodium, 34 g carbo., 2 g fiber, 7 g pro.
Daily Values: 4% vit. A, 16% calcium, 10% iron
Exchanges: 1 Starch, ½ Fat

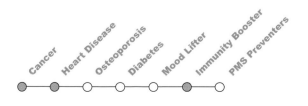

Cranberry Citrus Compote With Star Anise

Start to Finish: 25 minutes

Luscious, juicy oranges and tart cranberries soak in orange syrup seasoned with the sweet licorice flavor of anise. Vitamin C and flavenoids from citrus fruits and cranberries in this easy compote prevent cancer, forestall heart disease, and increase immunity.

  2 large oranges

1$\frac{1}{2}$ cups cranberries

  1 cup water

$\frac{2}{3}$ cup packed brown sugar

$\frac{1}{2}$ cup orange juice

  2 whole star anise

  2 large red grapefruit

1 Remove a 3×1-inch strip of peel from one of the oranges; set oranges aside. In a medium saucepan combine the strip of orange peel, cranberries, water, brown sugar, orange juice, and anise. Bring to boiling; reduce heat. Simmer, uncovered, for 5 minutes, stirring occasionally. Remove from heat. Transfer cranberry mixture to a medium bowl. Cool slightly. Discard orange peel and anise.

2 Meanwhile, peel, seed, and section the oranges and the grapefruit over a small bowl to catch juices. Stir orange and grapefruit sections and juices into the cranberry mixture. Serve compote warm or chilled. Makes 6 servings.

Nutrition Facts per serving: 148 cal., 0 g total fat (0 g sat. fat), 0 mg chol., 11 mg sodium, 37 g carbo., 3 g fiber, 1 g pro.
Daily Values: 5% vit. A, 83% vit. C, 5% calcium, 4% iron
Exchanges: 2$\frac{1}{2}$ Fruit

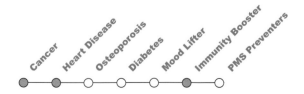

Dried Fruit Coffee Cake

Prep: 20 minutes **Bake:** 25 minutes

Sweet, tender coffee cake spiked with dried plums and dried apricots is a tasty way to add potassium and antioxidants to your diet. Potassium helps to regulate high blood pressure, and antioxidants help prevent heart disease.

Nonstick cooking spray	1 2$\frac{1}{2}$-ounce jar prune baby food or $\frac{1}{4}$ cup other prune
1$\frac{1}{2}$ cups all-purpose flour	puree product, or $\frac{1}{4}$ cup unsweetened applesauce
1 teaspoon baking powder	4 tablespoons butter, melted
$\frac{1}{4}$ teaspoon salt	1 teaspoon vanilla
1 slightly beaten egg	2 tablespoons sliced almonds
$\frac{1}{2}$ cup snipped dried plums (prunes)	2 tablespoons toasted wheat germ
$\frac{1}{4}$ cup snipped dried apricots	1 tablespoon brown sugar
$\frac{1}{2}$ cup packed brown sugar	

1 Lightly coat an 8×1$\frac{1}{2}$-inch round baking pan with cooking spray; set aside. In a small bowl stir together flour, baking powder, and salt.

2 In a medium bowl combine egg, snipped dried plums, and apricots. Stir in the $\frac{1}{2}$ cup brown sugar, the prune baby food, 3 tablespoons of the melted butter, and the vanilla. Add fruit mixture all at once to flour mixture; stir to combine. Pour batter into prepared baking pan.

3 For topping, in a small bowl stir together almonds, wheat germ, the 1 tablespoon brown sugar, and the remaining 1 tablespoon melted butter. Sprinkle the topping over batter; lightly press into batter.

4 Bake in a 350° oven for 25 to 30 minutes or until a toothpick inserted near the center comes out clean. Cool in pan on a wire rack for 10 minutes. Serve coffee cake warm. Makes 10 servings.

Nutrition Facts per serving: 207 cal., 7 g total fat (3 g sat. fat), 34 mg chol., 160 mg sodium, 35 g carbo., 2 g fiber, 4 g pro.
Daily Values: 13% vit. A, 1% vit. C, 5% calcium, 9% iron
Exchanges: $\frac{1}{2}$ Fruit, 1 Starch, 1 Fat

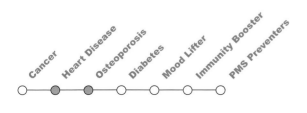

Raspberry and Cheese Coffee Cake, page 36

Raspberry And Cheese Coffee Cake

Prep: 20 minutes **Bake:** 30 minutes **Cool:** 10 minutes

This trimmed-down coffee cake stars fresh raspberries. The berries add brilliant color, flavor, and a little fiber, thanks to those tiny seeds. (Pictured on page 34.)

Nonstick cooking spray

1¼ cups all-purpose flour

1¼ teaspoons baking powder

1 teaspoon finely shredded lemon or orange peel

¼ teaspoon baking soda

¼ teaspoon salt

1 cup granulated sugar

3 tablespoons butter, softened

¼ cup refrigerated or frozen egg product, thawed

1 teaspoon vanilla

½ cup buttermilk

2 ounces reduced-fat cream cheese (Neufchâtel)

2 tablespoons refrigerated or frozen egg product, thawed

1 cup raspberries or thinly sliced apricots or nectarines*

Sifted powdered sugar

1 Lightly coat a 9×1½-inch round baking pan with cooking spray; set aside. In a medium bowl stir together flour, baking powder, lemon peel, baking soda, and salt.

2 In medium mixing bowl beat ¾ cup of the granulated sugar and the butter with an electric mixer on medium to high speed until combined. Add the ¼ cup egg product and the vanilla. Beat on low to medium speed for 1 minute. Alternately add flour mixture and buttermilk to egg mixture, beating just until combined after each addition. Pour batter into the prepared baking pan.

3 In a small bowl beat the cream cheese and the remaining ¼ cup granulated sugar on medium to high speed until combined. Add the 2 tablespoons egg product; beat until combined. Sprinkle raspberries over the batter in pan. Pour cream cheese mixture over raspberries, allowing some of the berries to show.

4 Bake in a 375° oven for 30 to 35 minutes or until a toothpick inserted near the center comes out clean. Cool in pan on a wire rack for 10 minutes. Dust with powdered sugar. Serve coffee cake warm. If desired, garnish each serving with additional raspberries. Makes 10 servings.

Nutrition Facts per serving: 195 cal., 5 g total fat (3 g sat. fat), 14 mg chol., 223 mg sodium, 33 g carbo., 1 g fiber, 4 g pro.
Daily Values: 11% vit. A, 2% vit. C, 5% calcium, 6% iron
Exchanges: 2 Starch, ½ Fat

*Note: If you like, substitute well drained, thinly sliced canned apricots or peach slices for the fresh fruit.

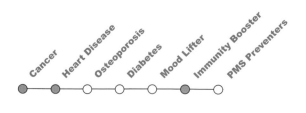

Creole-Style Grits   **Start to Finish:** 35 minutes

Full-flavored Creole seasoning, fresh asparagus, red sweet pepper, and onion impart flavors of French, Spanish, and African cuisines to this dish. The shrimp and vegetables offer nutrients to enhance immunity, boost energy, and safeguard against cancer, heart disease, and diabetes. (Pictured on page 35.)

1   pound fresh or frozen medium shrimp

$^{1}/_{2}$ cup quick-cooking yellow grits

12   ounces asparagus, trimmed and bias-sliced into 2-inch pieces

1   medium red sweet pepper, cut into $^{1}/_{2}$-inch squares

$^{1}/_{2}$ cup chopped onion

2   cloves garlic, minced

1   tablespoon olive oil

2   tablespoons all-purpose flour

2   teaspoons salt-free Creole seasoning

$^{3}/_{4}$ cup chicken broth

1 Thaw shrimp, if frozen. Peel and devein shrimp, leaving tails intact (if desired). Rinse shrimp; pat dry.

2 Prepare grits according to package directions. Cover and keep warm.

3 Meanwhile, in a large skillet cook asparagus, sweet pepper, onion, and garlic in hot oil for 4 to 5 minutes or just until vegetables are tender.

4 Stir flour and Creole seasoning into vegetable mixture. Add chicken broth. Cook and stir until mixture begins to bubble; reduce heat. Stir in shrimp. Cook, covered, for 1 to 3 minutes or until shrimp are opaque, stirring once. Serve shrimp mixture over grits. Makes 4 servings.

Nutrition Facts per serving: 243 cal., 6 g total fat (1 g sat. fat), 129 mg chol., 323 mg sodium, 25 g carbo., 2 g fiber, 22 g pro.
Daily Values: 36% vit. A, 105% vit. C, 6% calcium, 18% iron
Exchanges: 1 Vegetable, 1 Starch, 2$^{1}/_{2}$ Very Lean Meat, $^{1}/_{2}$ Fat

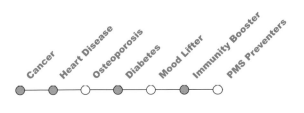

Fruit Granola

Prep: 20 minutes **Bake:** 25 minutes

Loaded with whole-grain nutrients such as fiber, vitamin E, and folate, this granola guards against heart disease, reduces the effects of menopause, enhances complexion, and helps control blood sugars. Serve the sweet, crunchy, fruit- and almond-studded cereal with your favorite yogurt for a great low-fat start to your day.

	Nonstick cooking spray	1$\frac{1}{2}$	teaspoons ground cinnamon
3	cups regular rolled oats (not quick-cooking)	$\frac{1}{3}$	cup orange juice
$\frac{1}{3}$	cup toasted wheat germ	$\frac{1}{3}$	cup honey
$\frac{1}{3}$	cup unsalted, shelled sunflower seeds	1	tablespoon cooking oil
$\frac{1}{3}$	cup sliced almonds	1	cup mixed dried fruit bits
3	tablespoons nonfat dry milk powder		Milk (optional)

1 Lightly coat a 15×10×1-inch baking pan with cooking spray; set aside. In a large bowl stir together oats, wheat germ, sunflower seeds, almonds, milk powder, and cinnamon.

2 In a small bowl stir together orange juice, honey, and oil. Pour juice mixture over oat mixture; toss to coat. Spread in the prepared baking pan.

3 Bake in a 325° oven about 25 minutes or until oats are light brown, stirring twice. Immediately turn out onto a large piece of foil. Stir in dried fruit bits. Cool completely.

4 To store, seal in storage bags and keep at room temperature for up to 2 weeks. For longer storage, seal in freezer bags and freeze. If desired, serve the granola with milk. Makes 10 servings.

Nutrition Facts per serving: 272 cal., 8 g total fat (1 g sat. fat), 0 mg chol., 18 mg sodium, 44 g carbo., 5 g fiber, 8 g pro.
Daily Values: 1% vit. A, 8% vit. C, 6% calcium, 12% iron
Exchanges: 1 Fruit, 2 Starch, 1 Fat

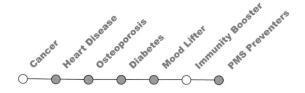

Oatmeal Brunch Casserole

Prep: 15 minutes **Bake:** 20 minutes

Oats have many things going for them. The soluble fiber in oats can help lower blood cholesterol levels and moderate blood sugar levels by slowing digestion. Oats, as well as walnuts, contain the antioxidant vitamin E.

Nonstick cooking spray

1¾ **cups vanilla-flavored soy milk or fat-free milk**

1 **tablespoon margarine or butter**

1 **cup regular rolled oats (not quick-cooking)**

1 **apple or pear, chopped**

⅓ **cup dried tart cherries or golden raisins**

¼ **cup coarsely chopped walnuts, toasted**

3 **tablespoons brown sugar**

½ **teaspoon vanilla (if using fat-free milk)**

¼ **teaspoon salt**

1 Lightly coat a 1½-quart casserole dish with cooking spray; set aside. In a medium saucepan bring the milk and margarine to boiling. Slowly stir in oats. Stir in apple, cherries, walnuts, 2 tablespoons of the brown sugar, the vanilla (if using), and salt. Cook and stir for 1 minute. Pour into the prepared casserole dish.

2 Bake, uncovered, in a 350° oven for 15 minutes. Sprinkle with the remaining 1 tablespoon brown sugar. Bake for 5 minutes more or until bubbly. Cool slightly. If desired, serve the warm oatmeal with additional milk. Makes 4 servings.

Nutrition Facts per serving: 316 cal., 11 g total fat (3 g sat. fat), 8 mg chol., 241 mg sodium, 47 g carbo., 4 g fiber, 8 g pro.
Daily Values: 7% vit. A, 4% vit. C, 16% calcium, 11% iron
Exchanges: ½ Milk, 1 Fruit, 1½ Starch, 1½ Fat

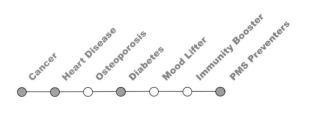

Fish Seafood

Grilled Salmon with Mango Salsa, page 42

Grilled Salmon With Mango Salsa

Prep: 15 minutes   **Marinate:** 4 hours   **Grill:** 20 minutes

Pack a dietary punch with this combination of salmon topped with mango salsa. The omega-3-rich fish increases immunity, fights heart disease, boosts energy levels, and lifts moods. The fiber-intensive mango contains generous amounts of vitamins A, C, and E. (Pictured on the cover and on page 41.)

4   6- to 8-ounce fresh or frozen salmon fillets (with skin), 1 inch thick

2   tablespoons sugar

1½ teaspoons finely shredded lime peel

¾   teaspoon salt

¼   teaspoon ground red pepper

1   large ripe mango, peeled, seeded, and cut into thin bite-size strips

½   of a medium cucumber, seeded and cut into thin bite-size strips

2   green onions, sliced

3   tablespoons lime juice

1   tablespoon snipped fresh cilantro or 2 teaspoons snipped fresh mint

1   small fresh jalapeño pepper, seeded and chopped*

1   clove garlic, minced

1 Thaw fish, if frozen. Rinse fish; pat dry. Place fish, skin side down, in a shallow dish.

2 For rub, in a small bowl stir together sugar, lime peel, ½ teaspoon of the salt, and the red pepper. Sprinkle rub evenly over fish; rub in with your fingers. Cover and marinate in the refrigerator for 4 to 24 hours.

3 Meanwhile, for salsa, in a medium bowl combine mango, cucumber, green onions, lime juice, cilantro, jalapeño pepper, garlic, and the remaining ¼ teaspoon salt. Cover and refrigerate until ready to serve.

4 In a grill with a cover arrange medium-hot coals around a drip pan. Test for medium heat above the pan. Place fish, skin side down, on the greased grill rack over the drip pan, tucking under any thin edges. Cover and grill for 20 to 25 minutes or until fish flakes easily with a fork. If desired, remove skin from fish. Serve the fish with salsa. Makes 4 servings.

Nutrition Facts per serving: 352 cal., 15 g total fat (3 g sat. fat), 105 mg chol., 520 mg sodium, 18 g carbo., 2 g fiber, 37 g pro.
Daily Values: 50% vit. A, 38% vit. C, 3% calcium, 6% iron
Exchanges: 1 Fruit, 5 Lean Meat

*Note: Hot peppers contain volatile oils in the seeds and inner membranes that can burn eyes, lips, and sensitive skin. Wear plastic gloves when handling hot peppers and wash your hands thoroughly with soap and water afterwards.

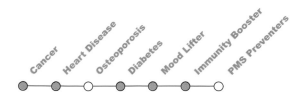

Sweet'n'Heat-Glazed Salmon

Prep: 30 minutes   **Broil:** 8 minutes

Fatty fish, such as salmon, mackerel, lake trout, herring, sardine, and albacore tuna, are high in omega-3 fatty acids. Research suggests that consuming omega-3s helps prevent heart disease and stroke. Apricots contain magnesium, a mineral that helps reduce the symptoms of PMS.

1½   **cups apricot nectar**

⅓   **cup snipped dried apricots**

2   **tablespoons honey**

2   **tablespoons reduced-sodium soy sauce**

1   **tablespoon grated fresh ginger**

2   **cloves garlic, minced**

¼   **teaspoon ground cinnamon**

⅛   **teaspoon ground red pepper**

1   **12-ounce fresh or frozen skinless salmon fillet, 1 inch thick**

1 For glaze, in a medium saucepan stir together apricot nectar, apricots, honey, soy sauce, ginger, garlic, cinnamon, and red pepper. Bring to boiling; reduce heat. Simmer, uncovered, about 20 minutes or until mixture is thickened and reduced by about half, stirring occasionally. Remove ¼ cup of the glaze for basting; set aside the remaining glaze until ready to serve.

2 Meanwhile, thaw fish, if frozen. Rinse fish; pat dry. Place fish on the greased, unheated rack of a broiler pan, tucking under any thin edges.

3 Broil about 4 inches from the heat for 8 to 12 minutes or until fish flakes easily with a fork, gently turning once and brushing occasionally with the ¼ cup glaze for the last 4 minutes of broiling. Serve the fish with the remaining glaze. Makes 4 servings.

Nutrition Facts per serving: 261 cal., 8 g total fat (1 g sat. fat), 52 mg chol., 332 mg sodium, 30 g carbo., 2 g fiber, 20 g pro.
Daily Values: 44% vit. A, 3% vit. C, 3% calcium, 8% iron
Exchanges: 2 Fruit, 3 Lean Meat

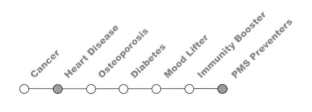

Pecan-Crusted Fish With Vegetables

Prep: 15 minutes **Bake:** 20 minutes

A crunchy pecan coating is the perfect foil for mild fish. The nuts and colorful vegetables provide a cornucopia of health-protective plant compounds such as vitamin E, vitamin C, carotenoids, and fiber.

Nonstick cooking spray	1 **egg**
12 **ounces fresh or frozen skinless catfish, whitefish, or orange roughy fillets, $^1/_2$ inch thick**	1 **tablespoon water**
$^1/_2$ **cup finely chopped pecans**	2 **small red and/or orange sweet peppers, quartered**
$^1/_3$ **cup yellow cornmeal**	1 **medium zucchini, bias-sliced $^1/_2$ inch thick**
$^1/_2$ **teaspoon onion salt**	1 **medium yellow summer squash, bias-sliced $^1/_2$ inch thick**
$^1/_4$ **cup all-purpose flour**	1 **tablespoon cooking oil**
$^1/_4$ **teaspoon ground red pepper**	$^1/_4$ **teaspoon seasoned salt**

1 Line a 15×10×1-inch baking pan with foil. Lightly coat the foil with cooking spray; set aside. Thaw fish, if frozen. Rinse fish; pat dry. Cut fish into 4 serving-size pieces; set aside.

2 In a shallow dish stir together pecans, cornmeal, and onion salt. In another shallow dish stir together flour and ground red pepper. In a small bowl beat together egg and water. Dip each piece of fish in flour mixture to coat lightly, shaking off any excess. Dip fish in egg mixture, then in pecan mixture to coat. Place coated fish in the prepared baking pan, tucking under any thin edges.

3 In a large bowl combine sweet peppers, zucchini, and summer squash. Add oil and seasoned salt; toss to coat. Arrange vegetables around fish, overlapping as needed to fit into the pan.

4 Bake, uncovered, in a 425° oven for 20 to 25 minutes or until the fish flakes easily with a fork and the vegetables are tender. Makes 4 servings.

Nutrition Facts per serving: 302 cal., 15 g total fat (2 g sat. fat), 98 mg chol., 367 mg sodium, 21 g carbo., 3 g fiber, 21 g pro.
Daily Values: 24% vit. A, 74% vit. C, 3% calcium, 12% iron
Exchanges: 1 Vegetable, 1 Starch, 2$^1/_2$ Lean Meat, 1 Fat

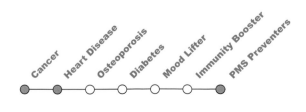

Blackened Snapper With Roasted Potatoes   **Prep:** 20 minutes   **Grill:** 35 minutes

Catch a pan-fried Cajun classic and cook it on your grill! This version of a Southern favorite is served alongside tiny new potatoes, carrots, and onions roasted in olive oil and zippy hot pepper sauce.

1   **tablespoon olive oil**

¼   **teaspoon salt**

    Several dashes bottled hot pepper sauce

1½   **pounds tiny new potatoes, thinly sliced**

4   **medium carrots, thinly sliced**

1   **medium green sweet pepper, cut into thin strips**

1   **medium onion, sliced**

4   **4- to 5-ounce fresh or frozen red snapper or catfish fillets, ½ to 1 inch thick**

½   **teaspoon Cajun seasoning**

    Nonstick spray coating

1   **tablespoon snipped fresh chervil or parsley**

1 Fold a 48×18-inch piece of heavy foil in half to make a 24×18-inch rectangle. In a large bowl combine the oil, salt, and hot pepper sauce. Add the potatoes, carrots, sweet pepper, and onion; toss to coat. Place in the center of foil. Bring up 2 opposite edges of foil; seal with a double fold. Fold remaining ends to completely enclose vegetables, leaving space for steam to build.

2 Grill vegetables on the rack of an uncovered grill directly over medium heat for 35 to 40 minutes or until potatoes and carrots are tender.

3 Meanwhile, thaw fish, if frozen. Rinse fish; pat dry. Sprinkle both sides of fish with Cajun seasoning and lightly spray with nonstick coating. Place fish in a well greased wire grill basket. Place the fish on the grill rack next to the vegetables and grill until fish flakes easily with a fork, turning the basket once. (Allow 4 to 6 minutes per ½-inch thickness of fish.) To serve, sprinkle fish and vegetables with snipped chervil. Makes 4 servings.

Nutrition Facts per serving: 352 cal., 6 g total fat (1 g sat. fat), 42 mg chol., 266 mg sodium, 48 g carbo., 5 g fiber, 28 g pro.
Daily Values: 173% vit. A, 63% vit. C, 7% calcium, 24% iron
Exchanges: 1 Vegetable, 2 Starch, 3½ Very Lean Meat

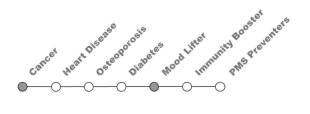

Tropical Seviche

Start to Finish: 35 minutes

Although seviche typically uses raw fish that is "cooked" in citrus juices, in this version the scallops are sauteed for safety reasons. This tasty medley is high in vitamin C, one of the most effective water-soluble antioxidants. It helps protect against heart disease and cancer, and it contributes to healthy eyes.

12 ounces fresh or frozen bay scallops	**2** cloves garlic, minced
1 large orange	**2** teaspoons olive oil
1 grapefruit	**1** large mango or papaya, peeled, seeded, and cubed
¼ cup finely chopped red onion	**2** tablespoons snipped fresh mint
1 fresh jalapeño pepper, seeded and finely chopped*	

1 Thaw scallops, if frozen. Rinse scallops; pat dry. Place scallops in a medium bowl.

2 For marinade, finely shred 1 teaspoon peel from the orange; set aside. Peel, seed, and section the orange and grapefruit over a small bowl to catch juices. Stir the orange peel, onion, jalapeño pepper, and garlic into the orange and grapefruit juices. Pour over scallops, stirring to coat. Cover and marinate at room temperature for 15 minutes. Drain scallop mixture, discarding marinade.

3 In a large skillet heat oil over medium-high heat. Add scallop mixture. Cook and stir for 1 to 2 minutes or until scallops are opaque. Transfer scallop mixture to another medium bowl; cool slightly. Drain and discard any liquid that has accumulated. Add the orange and grapefruit sections, mango, and mint to scallop mixture; toss gently to coat. Spoon into small bowls. If desired, garnish with additional mango. Makes 6 appetizer servings.

Nutrition Facts per serving: 99 cal., 2 g total fat (0 g sat. fat), 19 mg chol., 92 mg sodium, 10 g carbo., 1 g fiber, 10 g pro.
Daily Values: 24% vit. A, 46% vit. C, 3% calcium, 3% iron
Exchanges: ½ Fruit, 1½ Very Lean Meat

*Note: Hot peppers contain volatile oils in the seeds and inner membranes that can burn eyes, lips, and sensitive skin. Wear plastic gloves when handling hot peppers and wash your hands thoroughly with soap and water afterwards.

Cancer · Heart Disease · Osteoporosis · Diabetes · Mood Lifter · Immunity Booster · PMS Preventers

Wasabi-Glazed Cod With Vegetable Slaw

Prep: 15 minutes   **Grill:** 6 minutes

Thanks to wasabi, your taste buds won't soon forget this zingy fish dish. Similar to horseradish, wasabi is a fiery condiment made from the root of an Asian plant. The radishes in the slaw add more zip. They also add cancer-fighting compounds.

4   **4-ounce fresh or frozen cod, or orange roughy fillets, ³/₄ inch thick**

1   **medium zucchini, coarsely shredded (about 1¹/₃ cups)**

1   **cup sliced radishes**

1   **cup pea pods, strings removed**

3   **tablespoons snipped fresh chives**

3   **tablespoons rice vinegar**

1   **teaspoon toasted sesame oil**

¹/₂   **teaspoon sugar**

2   **tablespoons reduced-sodium soy sauce**

¹/₄   **teaspoon wasabi powder or 1 tablespoon prepared horseradish**

1 Thaw fish, if frozen. Rinse fish; pat dry. Set aside. For vegetable slaw, in a medium bowl combine zucchini, radishes, pea pods, and 2 tablespoons of the chives. Stir together vinegar, ¹/₂ teaspoon of the sesame oil, and ¹/₄ teaspoon of the sugar. Drizzle over zucchini mixture; toss to coat. Set aside until ready to serve.

2 In a small bowl combine the remaining ¹/₂ teaspoon sesame oil, the remaining ¹/₄ teaspoon sugar, the soy sauce, and wasabi powder. Brush soy mixture over both sides of fish. Place fish in a greased grill basket, tucking under any thin edges.

3 Grill fish on the rack of an uncovered grill directly over medium coals for 6 to 9 minutes or until fish flakes easily with a fork, turning basket once halfway through grilling.

4 To serve, sprinkle the remaining chives over fish. Serve the fish with vegetable slaw. Makes 4 servings.

Nutrition Facts per serving: 141 cal., 3 g total fat (1 g sat. fat), 60 mg chol., 363 mg sodium, 6 g carbo., 1 g fiber, 24 g pro.
Daily Values: 3% vit.A, 46% vit. C, 3% calcium, 10% iron
Exchanges: 1 Vegetable, 3¹/₂ Very Lean Meat

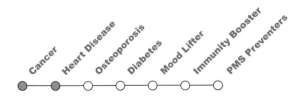

Linguine With Garlic Shrimp

Start to Finish: 55 minutes

The allium compounds that make garlic so pungent are also responsible for its potential to decrease blood cholesterol levels, reduce blood clotting and blood pressure, and fight cancer. Garlic's kissing cousins—onions, leeks, chives, and shallots—also contain allium compounds.

2 **large bulbs garlic**	2 **teaspoons cornstarch**
12 **ounces fresh or frozen peeled, deveined medium shrimp**	1½ **teaspoons snipped fresh oregano or ½ teaspoon**
8 **ounces dried plain and/or spinach linguine or fettuccine**	**dried oregano, crushed**
2 **cups sliced fresh mushrooms**	½ **teaspoon instant chicken bouillon granules**
1 **medium yellow or green sweet pepper, chopped**	⅛ **teaspoon black pepper**
1 **tablespoon olive oil or cooking oil**	2 **medium tomatoes, peeled, seeded, and chopped**
½ **cup water**	¼ **cup finely shredded Parmesan cheese**
1 **tablespoon snipped fresh basil or 1 teaspoon dried**	
basil, crushed	

1 For garlic paste, cut ½ inch off the pointed top portions of garlic bulbs. Remove the outer papery layers of the garlic. Place both bulbs on a square piece of foil. Bring edges of foil together to form a pouch; seal. Bake garlic in a 375° oven for 35 to 40 minutes or until very soft. When cool enough to handle, use your fingers to press garlic pulp from each clove. Mash pulp with a spoon or fork to make a smooth paste (you should have 2 to 3 tablespoons).

2 Meanwhile, thaw shrimp, if frozen. Rinse shrimp; pat dry. Set aside. Cook linguine according to package directions; drain. Return linguine to saucepan; cover and keep warm.

3 In a large saucepan cook mushrooms and sweet pepper in hot oil until pepper is tender. In a small bowl stir together the garlic paste, water, basil, cornstarch, oregano, bouillon granules, and black pepper. Add to mushroom mixture. Cook and stir until thickened and bubbly. Add shrimp to mushroom mixture. Simmer, covered, for 1 to 3 minutes or until shrimp are opaque. Stir in tomatoes; heat through.

4 To serve, spoon shrimp mixture over hot linguine. Sprinkle with Parmesan cheese; toss to combine. Makes 4 servings.

Nutrition Facts per serving: 357 cal., 7 g total fat (2 g sat. fat), 126 mg chol., 397 mg sodium, 49 g carbo., 6 g fiber, 24 g pro.
Daily Values: 16% vit. A, 173% vit. C, 23% calcium, 31% iron
Exchanges: 1 Vegetable, 3 Starch, 2½ Very Lean Meat

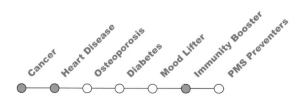

Cancer Heart Disease Osteoporosis Diabetes Mood Lifter Immunity Booster PMS Preventers

Tuna Salad Niçoise, page 52

Seared Scallops on Tropical Salsa, page 53

Tuna Salad Niçoise

Prep: 30 minutes   **Broil:** 8 minutes

Tuna is a terrific source of omega-3 fatty acids, which are polyunsaturated fats that help protect your heart. To reap the benefits, the American Heart Association recommends eating at least two servings of fish weekly. (Pictured on page 50.)

1 pound fresh or frozen tuna steaks, cut 1 inch thick	Black pepper
3 tablespoons sherry vinegar	8 ounces tiny new potatoes, quartered
2 tablespoons finely chopped shallots	6 ounces green beans
1 tablespoon Dijon-style mustard	6 cups Bibb or Boston lettuce leaves
2 tablespoons olive oil	¾ cup thinly sliced radishes
1 anchovy fillet, rinsed and mashed	½ cup niçoise olives, pitted (optional)
Salt	

1 Thaw fish, if frozen. Rinse fish; pat dry. For dressing, in a small bowl combine vinegar and shallots. Whisk in mustard. Add oil in a thin, steady stream, whisking constantly. Stir in the anchovy; season to taste with salt and black pepper. Remove 1 tablespoon of the dressing for brushing fish; set aside remaining dressing until ready to serve.

2 Brush the 1 tablespoon dressing over both sides of fish. Place fish on the greased, unheated rack of a broiler pan. Broil about 4 inches from the heat for 8 to 12 minutes or until fish flakes easily with a fork, gently turning once halfway through broiling. (Or grill fish on the greased rack of an uncovered grill directly over medium coals for 8 to 12 minutes, gently turning once halfway through grilling.) Cut fish into slices.

3 Meanwhile, in a medium saucepan cook potatoes in boiling water for 7 minutes. Add green beans; cook for 2 minutes more or until potatoes are tender. Drain and cool slightly.

4 To serve, arrange fish, potatoes, green beans, lettuce leaves, radishes, and, if desired, the olives on 4 dinner plates. Serve with the remaining dressing. Makes 4 servings.

Nutrition Facts per serving: 288 cal., 10 g total fat (1 g sat. fat), 51 mg chol., 413 mg sodium, 20 g carbo., 4 g fiber, 30 g pro.
Daily Values: 24% vit. A, 39% vit. C, 10% calcium, 17% iron
Exchanges: 2 Vegetable, ½ Starch, 3½ Very Lean Meat, 1½ Fat

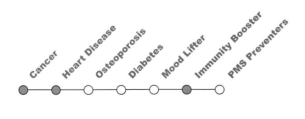

Seared Scallops With Tropical Salsa

Start to Finish: 25 minutes

Mild and sweet scallops get a tropical treatment with a colorful, zesty salsa. Scallops are nearly fat-free—3 ounces contain less than 1 gram of fat. This recipe is a great choice for light eating. It contains only 116 calories and 3 grams of fat. (Pictured on page 51.)

1 cup finely chopped strawberry papaya or papaya	1 teaspoon olive oil
½ cup seeded and finely chopped cucumber	12 ounces fresh or frozen scallops
1 small tomato, seeded and chopped	Salt
2 tablespoons snipped fresh cilantro	Black pepper
1 fresh jalapeño pepper, seeded and finely chopped*	1 clove garlic, minced
4 teaspoons lime juice	1 teaspoon margarine or butter

1 For salsa, in a small bowl stir together the papaya, cucumber, tomato, cilantro, jalapeño pepper, lime juice, and oil. Let stand at room temperature at least 15 minutes to allow flavors to blend.

2 Meanwhile, thaw scallops, if frozen. Rinse scallops and pat dry. Halve any large scallops. Lightly sprinkle scallops with salt and black pepper.

3 In a large nonstick skillet cook garlic in hot margarine over medium heat for 30 seconds. Add scallops. Cook and stir for 2 to 3 minutes or until scallops are opaque. Use a slotted spoon to remove scallops; drain on paper towels. Serve the scallops with salsa. Makes 4 servings.

Nutrition Facts per serving: 116 cal., 3 g total fat (0 g sat. fat), 28 mg chol., 151 mg sodium, 8 g carbo., 1 g fiber, 15 g pro.
Daily Values: 9% vit. A, 52% vit. C, 4% calcium, 2% iron
Exchanges: ½ Fruit, 2 Very Lean Meat

---

*Note: Hot peppers contain volatile oils in the seeds and inner membranes that can burn eyes, lips, and sensitive skin. Wear plastic gloves when handling hot peppers and wash your hands thoroughly with soap and water afterwards.

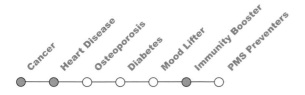

Spinach Risotto With Firecracker Shrimp   **Start to Finish:** 40 minutes

Shrimp is exceptionally low in fat, making it a great addition to a diet that protects against heart disease and cancer. Shrimp also offers iron and zinc, minerals important for energy and a healthy immune system.

1¼ cups arborio rice	⅛ teaspoon black pepper
1 tablespoon margarine or butter	12 ounces fresh or frozen peeled, deveined
2 14½-ounce cans reduced-sodium	medium shrimp
chicken broth	1 tablespoon olive oil
¾ cup dry white wine	2 cloves garlic, minced
1 cup chopped spinach	½ teaspoon crushed red pepper
⅛ teaspoon salt	¼ cup finely shredded Parmesan cheese

1 For risotto, in a medium nonstick saucepan cook and stir rice in hot margarine over medium heat for 5 minutes or until rice is golden brown. Carefully stir in broth and wine.

2 Bring to boiling; reduce heat. Simmer, covered, for 20 minutes. Remove from heat. Let stand, covered, for 5 minutes. Rice should be tender but slightly firm, and the mixture should be creamy. (If necessary, stir in a little water to reach desired consistency.) Stir in spinach, salt, and black pepper. Cover and keep warm.

3 Meanwhile, thaw shrimp, if frozen. Rinse shrimp; pat dry. In a large nonstick skillet heat oil over medium-high heat. Add shrimp, garlic, and red pepper. Cook and stir for 1 to 3 minutes or until shrimp are opaque.

4 To serve, divide risotto among 4 dinner plates. Spoon the shrimp over the risotto. Sprinkle each serving with Parmesan cheese. Makes 4 servings.

Nutrition Facts per serving: 363 cal., 10 g total fat (3 g sat. fat), 136 mg chol., 844 mg sodium, 36 g carbo., 0 g fiber, 25 g pro.
Daily Values: 16% vit. A, 6% vit. C, 12% calcium, 27% iron
Exchanges: 2½ Starch, 2½ Lean Meat

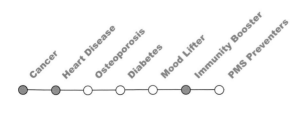

Fennel-Shrimp Chowder   **Start to Finish:** 30 minutes

Treat yourself to rich, creamy, low-fat chowder for lunch. The immunity-building shrimp pairs with tender, young asparagus spears and crisp red pepper to create an elegant soup bursting with antioxidants to fight cancer, diabetes, and heart disease.

12	ounces fresh or frozen, peeled and deveined medium shrimp
1	small fennel bulb
12	ounces asparagus spears
3	cups reduced-sodium chicken broth
1	cup chopped peeled potato
2/3	cup thinly sliced leeks
1/8	teaspoon salt
1/8	teaspoon black pepper
3/4	cup finely chopped red sweet pepper
1	cup fat-free half-and-half
2	tablespoons cornstarch

1 Thaw shrimp, if frozen. Rinse shrimp; pat dry. Cut off and discard upper stalks of fennel, reserving some of the feathery tops for garnish. Remove and discard any wilted tough outer layers of stalks. Cut off a thin slice from base of bulb; discard slice. Finely chop the bulb. Break off and discard woody bases of asparagus where spears snap easily. Scrape off scales. Cut asparagus into 1-inch pieces.

2 In a large saucepan combine chopped fennel, broth, potato, leeks, salt, and black pepper. Bring to boiling; reduce heat. Simmer, covered, for 8 minutes. Add shrimp, asparagus, and sweet pepper. Bring to boiling.

3 Combine half-and-half and cornstarch; add to shrimp mixture. Cook and stir until thickened and bubbly. Cook and stir for 2 minutes more or until shrimp are opaque. Garnish each serving with fennel leaves. Makes 4 servings.

Nutrition Facts per serving: 200 cal., 2 g total fat (0 g sat. fat), 97 mg chol., 717 mg sodium, 24 g carbo., 8 g fiber, 20 g pro.
Daily Values: 33% vit. A, 108% vit. C, 10% calcium, 14% iron
Exchanges: 2 Vegetable, 1 Starch, 2½ Very Lean Meat

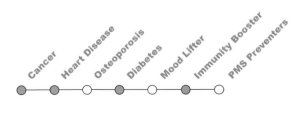

BeefPorkLamb

Beef Soup with Root Vegetables, page 58

Beef Soup With Root Vegetables

Prep: 25 minutes   **Cook:** 1½ hours

Potatoes, turnips, and sweet potatoes add a touch of sweetness to beef soup. They also pack in potassium and beta-carotene to control heart disease and supply a bevy of cancer-fighting nutrients. (Pictured on page 57.)

1 pound boneless beef round steak	1 cup water
2 tablespoons olive oil	2 sprigs fresh thyme
2 stalks celery, sliced	1 bay leaf
1 large onion, coarsely chopped	2 medium potatoes, peeled and cut into ¾-inch cubes
1 medium carrot, sliced	2 medium turnips, peeled and cut into ¾-inch cubes
2 cloves garlic, minced	1 large sweet potato, peeled and cut into ¾-inch cubes
2 14½-ounce cans beef broth	Flat crackers or crusty Italian bread (optional)

1 Trim fat from meat. Cut meat into ¾-inch cubes. In a 4-quart Dutch oven cook meat, half at a time, in 1 tablespoon of hot oil over medium heat until brown. Remove meat.

2 In the same Dutch oven heat the remaining 1 tablespoon oil over medium heat. Add celery, onion, carrot, and garlic; cook for 3 minutes, stirring frequently. Drain off any fat. Return meat to Dutch oven.

3 Stir in broth, water, thyme, and bay leaf. Bring to boiling; reduce heat. Simmer, covered, about 1¼ hours or until meat is nearly tender. Discard thyme and bay leaf. Stir in potatoes, turnips, and sweet potato. Bring to boiling; reduce heat. Simmer, covered, for 15 minutes more or until meat and vegetables are tender. If desired, serve the soup with crackers. Makes 6 servings.

Nutrition Facts per serving: 225 cal., 5 g total fat (1 g sat. fat), 30 mg chol., 551 mg sodium, 25 g carbo., 4 g fiber, 19 g pro.
Daily Values: 178% vit. A, 31% vit. C, 4% calcium, 13% iron
Exchanges: ½ Vegetable, 1½ Starch, 2½ Very Lean Meat

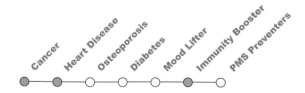

Beef And Rutabaga Stew

Prep: 25 minutes   **Cook:** 1½ hours

Ten cloves of garlic may sound overpowering, but it mellows with the slow simmer in the thyme-seasoned broth. The garlic in this hearty stew lowers cholesterol and teams with onion and rutabaga to protect against cancer.

12 ounces boneless beef chuck roast	10 cloves garlic
2 tablespoons all-purpose flour	1 bay leaf
1 cup chopped onion	½ teaspoon dried thyme, crushed
2 tablespoons olive oil or cooking oil	¼ teaspoon black pepper
1 14½-ounce can beef broth	1 pound rutabaga, peeled and cut into ¾-inch cubes
1 cup water	6 ounces green beans, trimmed and cut into 2½-inch pieces, or
½ cup dry red wine	1 cup loose-pack frozen cut green beans
1 tablespoon Worcestershire sauce	1 tablespoon tomato paste

1 Trim fat from meat. Cut meat into ¾-inch cubes. Place flour in a plastic bag. Add meat cubes, a few at a time, shaking to coat.

2 In a large saucepan or Dutch oven cook meat and onion in hot oil over medium heat for 4 to 5 minutes or until meat is brown. Drain off any fat. Stir in broth, water, wine, Worcestershire sauce, garlic, bay leaf, thyme, and black pepper. Bring to boiling; reduce heat. Simmer, covered, for 30 minutes.

3 Stir in rutabaga. Bring to boiling; reduce heat. Simmer, covered, for 1 hour more or until meat and rutabaga are tender, adding fresh green beans the last 20 minutes or frozen green beans the last 10 minutes of cooking. Discard bay leaf. Stir in tomato paste. Makes 4 or 5 servings.

Nutrition Facts per serving: 327 cal., 12 g total fat (3 g sat. fat), 40 mg chol., 514 mg sodium, 26 g carbo., 5 g fiber, 24 g pro.
Daily Values: 20% vit. A, 58% vit. C, 12% calcium, 22% iron
Exchanges: ½ Vegetable, 1½ Starch, 2½ Medium Fat Meat

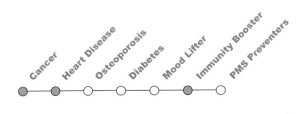

Curried Beef With Apple Couscous **Prep:** 20 minutes **Broil:** 10 minutes

This lively combination of curry and apples creates a noteworthy sauce for lean beef. The vitamin C and soluble fiber in this tasty entrée increase immunity, decrease the effects of menopause and arthritis, and help prevent heart disease, cancer, and diabetes.

10 ounces boneless beef top sirloin steak, cut 1 inch thick	1 medium onion, coarsely chopped
Salt	1 teaspoon cooking oil
Black pepper	1 tablespoon curry powder
1 tablespoon apple jelly	2 cups apple juice or water
1/2 teaspoon curry powder	1 tablespoon instant beef bouillon granules
2 medium tart green apples, chopped	1 10-ounce package quick-cooking couscous
1 medium red and/or green sweet pepper, cut into thin strips	1/3 cup chopped peanuts

1 Trim fat from meat. Lightly sprinkle meat with salt and black pepper. For glaze, in a small saucepan combine apple jelly and the 1/2 teaspoon curry powder. Cook and stir over medium heat until jelly is melted. (Or microwave in a microwave-safe bowl on 100% power [high] about 30 seconds.)

2 Place meat on the unheated rack of a broiler pan. Broil 3 to 4 inches from the heat until desired doneness, turning once and brushing occasionally with glaze the last 2 to 3 minutes of broiling. (Allow 10 to 12 minutes for medium doneness.)

3 Meanwhile, in a large skillet cook apples, sweet pepper, and onion in hot oil over medium heat for 5 minutes. Stir in the 1 tablespoon curry powder. Cook and stir for 1 minute. Add apple juice and bouillon granules. Bring to boiling. Stir in couscous; remove from heat. Cover and let stand about 5 minutes or until liquid is absorbed.

4 To serve, fluff couscous with a fork. Thinly slice meat across the grain. Serve meat on top of couscous. Sprinkle with peanuts. Makes 4 servings.

Nutrition Facts per serving: 506 cal., 11 g total fat (2 g sat. fat), 43 mg chol., 818 mg sodium, 74 g carbo., 8 g fiber, 29 g pro.
Daily Values: 31% vit. A, 83% vit. C, 5% calcium, 21% iron
Exchanges: 1/2 Vegetable, 1 Fruit, 3 1/2 Starch, 1 Medium Fat Meat

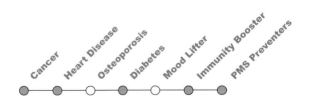

Pepper Steak With Horseradish Sauce   **Prep:** 20 minutes   **Grill:** 12 minutes

Tongue-twisting phytochemicals, called isothiocyanates, make horseradish hot and are among the most effective cancer-prevention agents known. Broccoli, cabbage, cauliflower, and kale also contain isothiocyanates.

$^1/_2$ **cup light mayonnaise dressing or salad dressing**

2   **tablespoons vinegar**

1   **tablespoon snipped fresh parsley**

1   **to 2 tablespoons prepared horseradish**

1   **to 1$^1/_2$ pounds beef flank steak or boneless beef top sirloin steak, cut 1 inch thick**

2   **teaspoons cracked black pepper**

1 For sauce, in a small bowl stir together mayonnaise dressing, vinegar, parsley, and horseradish. Set aside.

2 Trim fat from meat. If using flank steak, score both sides of meat in a diamond pattern by making shallow diagonal cuts at 1-inch intervals. Sprinkle both sides of meat with cracked black pepper, gently pressing into surface.

3 Grill meat on the rack of an uncovered grill directly over medium coals until desired doneness, turning once halfway through grilling. (Allow 12 to 15 minutes for medium doneness.) (Or broil on the unheated rack of a broiler pan 3 to 4 inches from the heat, turning once halfway through broiling. [Allow 12 to 15 minutes for medium doneness.])

4 To serve, thinly slice meat diagonally across the grain. Serve meat with sauce. Makes 4 to 6 servings.

Nutrition Facts per serving: 301 cal., 21 g total fat (7 g sat. fat), 68 mg chol., 253 mg sodium, 6 g carbo., 0 g fiber, 23 g pro.
Daily Values: 1% vit. A, 2% vit. C, 1% calcium, 14% iron
Exchanges: 3$^1/_2$ Medium Fat Meat, 1 Fat

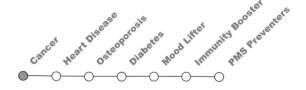

Beef And Black Bean Wraps

Start to Finish: 25 minutes

Whole wheat tortillas and black beans make this sandwich a filling, high-fiber meal with a snappy, south-of-the-border appeal. It safeguards against diabetes, strengthens the immune system, and protects against some cancers.

8 ounces lean ground beef	1 large tomato, chopped
1 cup chopped onion	1/4 teaspoon salt
2 cloves garlic, minced	1/4 teaspoon black pepper
1 1/2 teaspoons ground cumin	6 8-inch whole wheat flour tortillas
1 teaspoon chili powder	1 1/2 cups shredded lettuce
1/2 teaspoon ground coriander	1 to 1 1/2 cups shredded cheddar or Monterey Jack
1 15-ounce can black beans, rinsed	cheese (4 to 6 ounces)
and drained	Salsa (optional)

1 In a large skillet cook ground beef, onion, and garlic for 5 minutes or until meat is brown. Drain off fat.

2 Stir in cumin, chili powder, and coriander. Cook and stir for 1 minute. Stir in black beans, tomato, salt, and black pepper. Cook, covered, for 5 minutes more, stirring occasionally.

3 To serve, spoon beef mixture down the center of each tortilla. Sprinkle with lettuce and cheese. Roll up. If desired, serve with salsa. Makes 6 servings.

Nutrition Facts per serving: 267 cal., 10 g total fat (5 g sat. fat), 44 mg chol., 593 mg sodium, 27 g carbo., 14 g fiber, 19 g pro.
Daily Values: 18% vit. A, 19% vit. C, 20% calcium, 11% iron
Exchanges: 1 1/2 Starch, 2 1/2 Medium Fat Meat

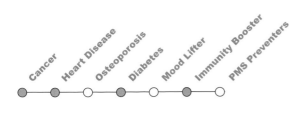

Steak Salad with Buttermilk Dressing, page 67

Flank Steak with Corn Salsa, page 66

Flank Steak With Corn Salsa

Prep: 15 minutes   **Marinate:** 6 hours   **Broil:** 12 minutes

Beef, lamb, and some dairy products contain a type of polyunsaturated fat called conjugated linoleic acid (CLA). Preliminary research suggests that CLA may help decrease the risk of cancer, heart disease, and type 2 diabetes. It may also help reduce body fat. Stay tuned as CLA research unfolds. (Pictured on page 65.)

1   **8³⁄₄-ounce can whole kernel corn, drained**

³⁄₄   **cup salsa verde**

1   **medium tomato, chopped**

1   **1¹⁄₄- to 1¹⁄₂-pound beef flank steak**

³⁄₄   **cup Italian salad dressing**

2   **tablespoons cracked black pepper**

1   **tablespoon Worcestershire sauce**

1   **teaspoon ground cumin**

1 For salsa, in a medium bowl combine corn, salsa verde, and tomato. Cover and refrigerate for 6 to 24 hours.

2 Meanwhile, trim fat from meat. Score both sides of meat in a diamond pattern by making shallow diagonal cuts at 1-inch intervals. Place meat in a plastic bag set in a shallow dish.

3 For marinade, in a small bowl combine salad dressing, black pepper, Worcestershire sauce, and cumin. Pour over meat; seal bag. Marinate in the refrigerator for 6 to 24 hours, turning bag occasionally. Drain meat, discarding marinade.

4 Place meat on the unheated rack of a broiler pan. Broil 3 to 4 inches from the heat until desired doneness, turning once halfway through broiling. (Allow 12 to 15 minutes for medium doneness.)

5 To serve, thinly slice meat diagonally across the grain. Serve meat with salsa. Makes 6 servings.

Nutrition Facts per serving: 197 cal., 10 g total fat (0 g sat. fat), 44 mg chol., 313 mg sodium, 9 g carbo., 2 g fiber, 19 g pro.
Daily Values: 19% vit. C, 14% iron
Exchanges: ¹⁄₂ Starch, 3 Lean Meat

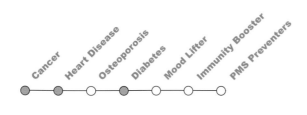

Steak Salad With Buttermilk Dressing

Start to Finish: 30 minutes

Beef is one of the best sources of iron and zinc, two minerals in which many women are deficient. Choose deeply colored mixed greens for the most flavor and phytochemicals. (Pictured on page 64.)

1   recipe Buttermilk Dressing

8   cups torn, mixed salad greens

2   medium carrots, cut into thin bite-size strips

1   medium yellow sweet pepper, cut into thin bite-size strips

1   cup cherry or pear-shaped tomatoes, halved

8   ounces boneless beef top sirloin steak

    Nonstick cooking spray

1/4   cup finely shredded fresh basil

1 Prepare Buttermilk Dressing. Arrange salad greens, carrots, sweet pepper, and tomatoes on 4 dinner plates. Set aside. Trim fat from meat. Cut meat across the grain into thin bite-size strips.

2 Lightly coat a large skillet with cooking spray. Heat over medium-high heat. Add meat. Cook and stir for 2 to 3 minutes or until meat is slightly pink in the center. Remove from heat. Stir in basil. Sprinkle with additional salt and black pepper to taste.

3 To serve, spoon the warm meat mixture over greens mixture. Drizzle each serving with Buttermilk Dressing. Serve immediately. Makes 4 servings.

Buttermilk Dressing: In a small bowl combine 1/2 cup plain low-fat yogurt; 1/3 cup buttermilk; 3 tablespoons freshly grated Parmesan cheese; 3 tablespoons finely chopped red onion; 3 tablespoons light mayonnaise dressing or salad dressing; 2 tablespoons snipped fresh parsley; 1 tablespoon white wine vinegar or lemon juice; 1 clove garlic, minced; 1/4 teaspoon salt; and 1/8 teaspoon black pepper. Cover and refrigerate at least 30 minutes or until ready to serve.

Nutrition Facts per serving: 226 cal., 10 g total fat (4 g sat. fat), 32 mg chol., 387 mg sodium, 17 g carbo., 4 g fiber, 19 g pro.
Daily Values: 206% vit. A, 181% vit. C, 20% calcium, 13% iron
Exchanges: 3 Vegetable, 2 Lean Meat, 1/2 Fat

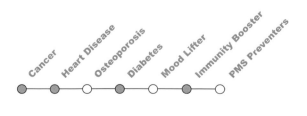

Grilled Lamb and Bulgur Burgers, page 70

Lamb Kabobs with Mustard Glaze, page 71

Grilled Lamb And Bulgur Burgers   **Prep:** 20 minutes   **Bake:** 20 minutes

Garlic, coriander, and thyme season these juicy lamb and bulgur burgers. For the low-fat option, ask your butcher to grind leg of lamb; otherwise select the leanest ground lamb available. Lean lamb provides iron, niacin, B vitamins, and zinc to fight infections and prevent anemia.

1 8-ounce carton plain low-fat yogurt	1 teaspoon ground coriander
2 teaspoons snipped fresh dill or ½ teaspoon dried dillweed	1 teaspoon snipped fresh thyme or ¼ teaspoon dried thyme, crushed
¾ cup water	⅛ teaspoon black pepper
½ cup bulgur	12 ounces lean ground lamb
½ teaspoon salt	½ of a medium cucumber, cut lengthwise into thin ribbons
¼ cup finely chopped onion	6 sandwich rolls or whole wheat hamburger buns, split
3 tablespoons snipped fresh parsley	Tomato slices (optional)
2 cloves garlic, minced	

1 For sauce, in a small bowl stir together yogurt and dill. Cover and refrigerate until ready to serve.

2 In a small saucepan bring water to boiling. Stir in bulgur and ¼ teaspoon of the salt. Reduce heat to low. Cook, covered, for 10 minutes. Remove from heat. Let stand, covered, for 5 minutes.

3 Meanwhile, in a large bowl combine the onion, parsley, garlic, coriander, thyme, black pepper, and the remaining ¼ teaspoon salt. Stir in cooked bulgur and ground lamb; mix well. Shape meat mixture into six ½-inch-thick patties. Place in a shallow baking pan. Bake in a 350° oven for 20 to 25 minutes or until meat is done (160°).

4 To serve, arrange the cucumber ribbons on bottoms of rolls. Add burgers, sauce, tomato slices (if desired), and roll tops. Makes 6 servings.

Nutrition Facts per serving: 295 cal., 11 g total fat (4 g sat. fat), 40 mg chol., 454 mg sodium, 32 g carbo., 4 g fiber, 18 g pro.
Daily Values: 3% vit. A, 7% vit. C, 13% calcium, 16% iron
Exchanges: 2 Starch, 2 Medium Fat Meat

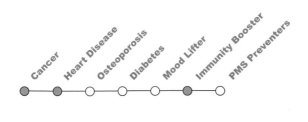

Lamb Kabobs With Mustard Glaze

Prep: 20 minutes **Marinate:** 2 hours **Grill:** 12 minutes

Pungent mustard and savory thyme glaze lean chunks of lamb and vegetables in these grilled kabobs. The colorful entrée provides plenty of vitamin C, B vitamins, iron, and zinc, making it great for boosting immunity, fighting heart disease, defending against cancer, and helping control blood sugar. (Pictured on page 69.)

12	ounces lean boneless lamb leg
1/4	cup Dijon-style mustard
3	tablespoons lemon juice
1	green onion, finely chopped
2	teaspoons snipped fresh thyme or 1/2 teaspoon dried thyme, crushed
16	tiny new potatoes, halved (about 1 1/4 pounds)
1	small red onion, cut into wedges
1	red, yellow, or green sweet pepper, cut into 1 1/2-inch squares
	Hot cooked orzo (optional)

1 Trim fat from meat. Cut meat into 1-inch cubes. Place meat in a medium bowl.

2 For marinade, in a small bowl stir together mustard, lemon juice, green onion, and thyme. Pour half the marinade over meat, stirring to coat. Cover and marinate in the refrigerator for 2 to 6 hours, stirring occasionally. Cover and refrigerate the remaining marinade for glaze.

3 Before grilling, place a steamer basket in a large saucepan. Add water to just below the bottom of the steamer basket. Bring to boiling. Add potatoes. Steam, covered, for 10 to 12 minutes or just until potatoes are tender. Remove steamer basket from saucepan; cool potatoes for 5 minutes. Break each onion wedge into 2 or 3 layers. Drain meat, discarding marinade.

4 On eight 6- to 8-inch metal skewers alternately thread meat, potatoes, onion, and sweet pepper, leaving 1/4 inch between pieces. Grill kabobs on the rack of an uncovered grill directly over medium coals for 12 to 14 minutes or until meat is slightly pink in the center, turning and brushing occasionally with glaze up to the last 5 minutes of grilling. (Or broil on the unheated rack of a broiler pan 3 to 4 inches from the heat for 6 to 8 minutes, turning and brushing occasionally with glaze up to the last 5 minutes of broiling.) If desired, serve kabobs with orzo. Makes 4 servings.

Nutrition Facts per serving: 408 cal., 22 g total fat (9 g sat. fat), 78 mg chol., 139 mg sodium, 28 g carbo., 4 g fiber, 24 g pro.
Daily Values: 31% vit. A, 120% vit. C, 5% calcium, 20% iron
Exchanges: 1/2 Vegetable, 1 1/2 Starch, 3 Medium Fat Meat, 1 Fat

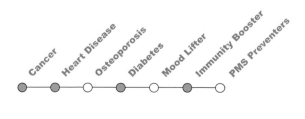

Lamb With Two-Pepper Bulgur

Prep: 15 minutes   **Broil:** 7 minutes

Bulgur, made from steamed, dried, and crushed wheat kernels, possesses a nutty flavor and chewy texture. Eating whole-grain foods such as bulgur may reduce the risk of heart disease and cancers of the lung, colon, esophagus, and stomach.

- 2 **cups water**
- 1 **cup bulgur**
- ½ **cup chopped onion**
- 4 **lamb loin chops, cut 1 inch thick (about 1 pound total)**
- 1½ **teaspoons lemon-pepper seasoning**
- 1 **cup small spinach leaves or shredded spinach**
- 1 **7-ounce jar roasted red sweet peppers, drained and coarsely chopped**

1 In a medium saucepan combine water, bulgur, and onion. Bring to boiling; reduce heat. Simmer, covered, for 12 to 15 minutes or until most of the liquid is absorbed. Drain. Cover and keep warm.

2 Meanwhile, trim fat from meat. Sprinkle meat with ½ teaspoon of the lemon-pepper seasoning. Place meat on the unheated rack of a broiler pan. Broil 3 to 4 inches from the heat until desired doneness, turning once halfway through broiling. (Allow 7 to 11 minutes for medium doneness.)

3 To serve, stir the remaining 1 teaspoon lemon-pepper seasoning, the spinach, and roasted peppers into bulgur mixture. Divide bulgur mixture among 4 dinner plates. Top with lamb chops. Makes 4 servings.

Nutrition Facts per serving: 396 cal., 22 g total fat (9 g sat. fat), 69 mg chol., 476 mg sodium, 31 g carbo., 8 g fiber, 20 g pro.
Daily Values: 8% vit. A, 175% vit. C, 4% calcium, 17% iron
Exchanges: ½ Vegetable, 2 Starch, 2½ Medium Fat Meat

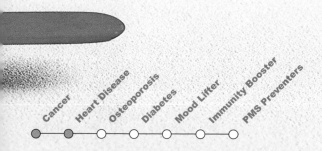

Cancer   Heart Disease   Osteoporosis   Diabetes   Mood Lifter   Immunity Booster   PMS Preventers

Lamb Loin With Pomegranate Compote

Prep: 25 minutes   **Roast:** 25 minutes   **Stand:** 10 minutes

The essence of mint heightens the flavors of this sparkling compote with pomegranate seeds and orange sections. Potassium-loaded pomegranate teams with vitamin-C-rich oranges to help lower blood pressure, prevent cancer, promote immunity, abate menopause symptoms, temper diabetes, and augment energy.

2 medium oranges	1 boneless lamb loin roast (about 1 pound)
1 tablespoon snipped fresh mint	4 cloves garlic, minced
1 tablespoon rice vinegar	2 tablespoons snipped fresh parsley
1 tablespoon mint jelly	1/4 teaspoon salt
1/2 cup chopped, seeded cucumber	1/4 teaspoon black pepper
2 tablespoons pomegranate seeds or snipped dried cranberries	1 tablespoon olive oil

1 For compote, peel, seed, and section the oranges over a small bowl to catch juice. Reserve 2 tablespoons of the juice in bowl. Whisk in mint, vinegar, and jelly. Stir in the orange sections, cucumber, and pomegranate seeds. Cover and refrigerate for up to 2 hours.

2 Trim fat from meat. Place meat between 2 pieces of plastic wrap. Working from the center to the edges, use the flat side of a meat mallet to pound meat to 1/2-inch thickness. Remove plastic wrap. Rub garlic over meat; sprinkle with parsley, salt, and black pepper. Starting from a long side, roll up into a spiral. Tie with 100-percent-cotton string at 1 1/2-inch intervals. Lightly sprinkle with salt and black pepper.

3 In a large ovenproof skillet cook meat in hot oil until evenly brown on all sides. Insert a meat thermometer into the center of meat. Place skillet in a 400° oven. Roast for 25 to 30 minutes or until the thermometer registers 155° for medium doneness. Remove meat from oven.

4 Cover meat with foil; let stand for 10 minutes. (The internal temperature will rise about 5° during standing.) To serve, cut meat into 1/2-inch slices. Serve meat with compote. Makes 4 servings.

Nutrition Facts per serving: 204 cal., 10 g total fat (3 g sat. fat), 56 mg chol., 81 mg sodium, 11 g carbo., 1 g fiber, 18 g pro.
Daily Values: 4% vit. A, 43% vit. C, 4% calcium, 12% iron
Exchanges: 1/2 Fruit, 2 1/2 Medium Fat Meat

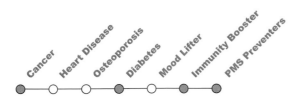

Cancer   Heart Disease   Osteoporosis   Diabetes   Mood Lifter   Immunity Booster   PMS Preventers

Lamb And Garbanzo Bean Curry

Start to Finish: 45 minutes

This lamb, garbanzo beans, tomato, and spinach jumble is simmered with aromatic curry to make a welcome dinner on cold winter nights. It will warm with homey flavors and fortify you with a wealth of nutrients. Full of many phytochemicals, it will help you ward off a myriad of ills.

12	ounces boneless lamb shoulder roast
2	tablespoons all-purpose flour
$^1/_4$	teaspoon salt
1	cup chopped onion
1	clove garlic, minced
2	tablespoons cooking oil
1	tablespoon curry powder
$1^1/_2$	cups reduced-sodium chicken broth
1	15-ounce can garbanzo beans, rinsed and drained
1	$14^1/_2$-ounce can tomatoes, undrained and cut up
4	cups coarsely chopped spinach

1 Trim fat from meat. Cut meat into 1-inch pieces. In a plastic bag combine flour and salt. Add meat pieces, a few at a time, shaking to coat.

2 In a large saucepan or Dutch oven cook onion and garlic in hot oil over medium heat for 4 minutes or until onion is tender. Add meat. Cook for 4 to 5 minutes or until meat is brown. Stir in curry powder. Cook and stir for 30 seconds more.

3 Add broth. Bring to boiling; reduce heat. Simmer, covered, for 20 minutes, stirring occasionally. Stir in garbanzo beans and tomatoes. Bring to boiling; reduce heat. Simmer, covered, for 10 minutes more or until meat is tender, stirring occasionally. Remove from heat. Add spinach, stirring just until wilted. Serve immediately. Makes 4 or 5 servings.

Nutrition Facts per serving: 413 cal., 23 g total fat (7 g sat. fat), 58 mg chol., 954 mg sodium, 28 g carbo., 10 g fiber, 24 g pro.
Daily Values: 57% vit. A, 45% vit. C, 13% calcium, 35% iron
Exchanges: 2 Vegetable, 1 Starch, 3 Medium Fat Meat, 1 Fat

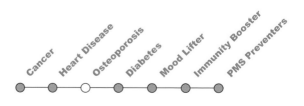

Lamb Chops With Mashed Celeriac

Prep: 25 minutes **Marinate:** 1 hour **Grill:** 10 minutes

Celeriac flavors creamy mashed potatoes with gentle hints of celery and parsley, making it the perfect accompaniment to these rosemary- and lemon-scented lamb chops. Phenolic compounds found in celeriac fight cancer and heart disease.

8   lamb loin chops, cut 1 inch thick ($1\frac{1}{2}$ to $1\frac{3}{4}$ pounds total)

Salt

Black pepper

3   tablespoons sherry vinegar or white wine vinegar

3   tablespoons olive oil

1   tablespoon snipped fresh rosemary or $\frac{1}{2}$ teaspoon dried rosemary, crushed

2   cloves garlic, minced

1   teaspoon finely shredded lemon peel

3   medium potatoes, peeled and quartered (1 pound)

8   ounces celeriac (celery root), peeled and cut into 1-inch cubes

1   to 2 teaspoons olive oil (optional)

$\frac{1}{4}$ teaspoon salt

$\frac{1}{8}$ teaspoon black pepper

$\frac{1}{4}$ to $\frac{1}{2}$ cup milk or chicken broth, warmed

1 Trim fat from meat. Sprinkle meat with salt and black pepper. Place meat in a plastic bag set in a shallow dish. For marinade, in a small bowl combine vinegar, the 3 tablespoons oil, the rosemary, garlic, and lemon peel. Pour over meat; seal bag. Marinate in the refrigerator for 1 to 4 hours, turning bag occasionally.

2 Before grilling, in a medium covered saucepan cook potatoes and celeriac in boiling, lightly salted water for 15 to 20 minutes or until vegetables are tender; drain. Use a ricer or potato masher to mash vegetables. Stir in 1 to 2 teaspoons oil (if desired), salt, and pepper. Stir in enough of the milk to make the vegetables light and fluffy. Cover and keep warm.

3 Drain meat, discarding marinade. Grill meat on the rack of an uncovered grill directly over medium coals until desired doneness, turning once halfway through grilling. (Allow 10 to 14 minutes for medium-rare and 14 to 16 minutes for medium doneness.) Serve lamb chops with mashed vegetables. Makes 4 servings.

Nutrition Facts per serving: 429 cal., 20 g total fat (5 g sat. fat), 84 mg chol., 254 mg sodium, 23 g carbo., 3 g fiber, 29 g pro.
Daily Values: 1% vit. A, 31% vit. C, 7% calcium, 20% iron
Exchanges: $1\frac{1}{2}$ Starch, 3 Medium Fat Meat, 1 Fat

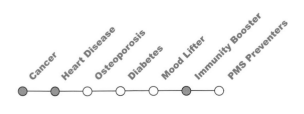

Grilled Pork And Pepper Skewers

Prep: 20 minutes   **Marinate:** 4 hours   **Grill:** 12 minutes

Smoky chipotle peppers complement peppery, sweet ginger and spicy coriander in the yogurt-based marinade on these lean pork, onion, and sweet pepper kabobs. They add plenty of vitamin C, B vitamins, iron, and zinc to your diet, helping to protect against many diseases as well as improve moods.

12 ounces boneless pork top loin roast	**1 tablespoon grated fresh ginger**
2 medium red sweet peppers, cut into 1-inch squares	**2 cloves garlic, minced**
1 medium red onion, cut into 1-inch pieces	**1 teaspoon sugar**
1 8-ounce carton plain low-fat yogurt	**1 teaspoon ground coriander**
3 green onions, thinly sliced	**¼ teaspoon salt**
2 chipotle peppers in adobo sauce, finely chopped	**⅛ teaspoon black pepper**
2 tablespoons snipped fresh parsley	**Hot cooked brown rice (optional)**

1 Trim fat from meat. Cut meat into 1-inch pieces. Place meat, sweet peppers, and red onion in a medium bowl.

2 For marinade, in a small bowl stir together yogurt, green onions, chipotle peppers, parsley, ginger, garlic, sugar, coriander, salt, and black pepper. Pour over meat mixture, stirring to coat. Cover and marinate in the refrigerator for 4 to 6 hours, stirring occasionally.

3 When assembling the kabobs, wear plastic or rubber gloves to protect your hands from the oils in the chipotle peppers. On eight 6- to 8-inch metal skewers alternately thread meat, sweet peppers, and red onion, leaving ¼ inch between pieces.

4 Grill kabobs on the rack of an uncovered grill directly over medium coals for 12 to 14 minutes or until meat is slightly pink in the center, turning once halfway through grilling. If desired, serve the kabobs with rice. Makes 4 servings.

Nutrition Facts per serving: 184 cal., 3 g total fat (1 g sat. fat), 53 mg chol., 298 mg sodium, 14 g carbo., 2 g fiber, 24 g pro.
Daily Values: 68% vit. A, 173% vit. C, 13% calcium, 10% iron
Exchanges: ½ Milk, 1 Vegetable, 2½ Lean Meat

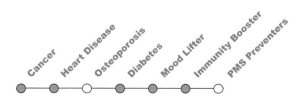

Pork Tenderloin over Red Cabbage, page 80

Pork with Black Beans and Succotash, page 81

Pork Tenderloin Over Red Cabbage

Prep: 20 minutes   **Roast:** 25 minutes   **Stand:** 10 minutes

Lean pork tenderloin shares top billing with cancer-fighting red cabbage. Cabbage and other cruciferous vegetables, such as broccoli, Brussels sprouts, cauliflower, kale, and collards, are thought to stimulate the body's production of anticancer enzymes. (Pictured on page 78.)

1	12-ounce pork tenderloin	½	cup white wine vinegar
	Salt	2	teaspoons brown sugar
	Black pepper	1	cup reduced-sodium chicken broth
1	medium red onion, cut into thin wedges	⅓	cup golden raisins
1	tablespoon olive oil	2	teaspoons snipped fresh thyme or ½ teaspoon
3	cups shredded red cabbage		dried thyme, crushed
⅓	cup white wine vinegar	1	tablespoon cornstarch
½	teaspoon salt	1	tablespoon cold water
¼	teaspoon black pepper	¼	cup coarsely chopped nuts, toasted

1 Place meat on a rack in a shallow roasting pan. Sprinkle with salt and black pepper. Insert a meat thermometer into the center of meat. Roast in a 425° oven for 25 to 35 minutes or until thermometer registers 155°. Remove meat from the oven. Cover meat with foil; let stand for 10 minutes. (The internal temperature will rise about 5° during standing.)

2 Meanwhile, for cabbage mixture, in a large skillet cook onion in hot oil over medium heat for 4 minutes or until tender. Add cabbage. Cook for 5 minutes, stirring occasionally. Stir in the ⅓ cup vinegar, ¼ teaspoon of the salt, and ⅛ teaspoon of the black pepper. Bring to boiling; reduce heat to low. Cook, covered, for 10 minutes or until cabbage is tender, stirring occasionally.

3 For sauce, in a small saucepan bring the ½ cup vinegar, the brown sugar, remaining ¼ teaspoon salt, and remaining ⅛ teaspoon black pepper to boiling. Boil gently, uncovered, for 6 minutes or until vinegar mixture is reduced by about half. Stir in broth, raisins, and thyme. Bring to boiling; reduce heat. In a small bowl combine cornstarch and water; add to vinegar mixture. Cook and stir until thickened and bubbly. Cook and stir for 2 minutes more.

4 To serve, slice meat diagonally into ½-inch slices. Divide the cabbage mixture among 4 dinner plates. Top with the meat slices and drizzle with sauce. Sprinkle with nuts. Makes 4 servings.

Nutrition Facts per serving: 272 cal., 10 g total fat (2 g sat. fat), 50 mg chol., 527 mg sodium, 20 g carbo., 3 g fiber, 24 g pro.
Daily Values: 1% vit. A, 47% vit. C, 5% calcium, 12% iron
Exchanges: 1 Vegetable, 1 Fruit, 3 Lean Meat

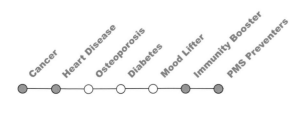

Pork With Black Beans And Succotash   **Start to Finish:** 20 minutes

Southwestern-style dishes such as this one often get their spicy taste from salsa. Tomato-based salsas contain the powerful antioxidant lycopene, which might help reduce prostate cancer risk. (Pictured on page 79.)

8   **to 10$\frac{1}{2}$ ounces low-fat bulk pork sausage**

$\frac{1}{2}$ **cup chopped onion**

$\frac{1}{2}$ **cup chopped red sweet pepper**

1   **10-ounce package frozen succotash or 1 cup frozen whole kernel corn plus 1 cup frozen lima beans**

$\frac{1}{4}$ **cup water**

1   **15-ounce can black beans, rinsed and drained**

$\frac{1}{2}$ **cup salsa**

2   **tablespoons snipped fresh cilantro**

8   **6-inch corn tortillas**

1   **small avocado, seeded, peeled, and sliced**

Light dairy sour cream (optional)

1 In a large nonstick skillet cook sausage, onion, and sweet pepper for 5 minutes or until meat is brown. Drain off fat. Stir in succotash and water.

2 Bring to boiling; reduce heat. Simmer, covered, for 15 minutes or until beans in succotash are tender. Stir in black beans and salsa. Heat through. Remove from heat. Stir in cilantro.

3 Meanwhile, wrap tortillas in foil. Heat in a 350° oven about 10 minutes or until warm. Serve sausage mixture with tortillas, avocado slices (halved), and, if desired, sour cream. Makes 4 servings.

Nutrition Facts per serving: 392 cal., 5 g total fat (1 g sat. fat), 33 mg chol., 717 mg sodium, 66 g carbo., 10 g fiber, 24 g pro.
Daily Values: 27% vit. A, 60% vit. C, 13% calcium, 25% iron
Exchanges: 4 Starch, 1$\frac{1}{2}$ Lean Meat

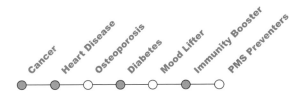

Harvest Pork Soup   **Start to Finish:** 30 minutes

Slightly sweet, hearty root vegetables—carrot, sweet potato, and turnip—complement tender chunks of pork in this herbed soup. The hot soup chases off the chill of fall days and fights cancer and heart disease. It also increases immunity, boosts energy, and lessens menopause symptoms.

10 ounces boneless pork top loin chops, cut ¾ inch thick	1 cup chopped, peeled turnip
1 tablespoon cooking oil	½ cup sliced celery
5 cups beef or chicken broth	½ cup quick-cooking pearl barley
2 cups cubed, peeled sweet potatoes	1 tablespoon snipped fresh oregano or ½ teaspoon dried oregano, crushed
1 cup sliced carrots	1 tablespoon snipped fresh sage or ½ teaspoon ground sage
1 cup chopped onion	¼ teaspoon black pepper

1 Trim fat from pork chops. Cut pork chops into ¾-inch pieces. In a 4-quart Dutch oven cook pork pieces in hot oil over medium heat for 4 to 5 minutes or until brown. Drain off any fat.

2 Add broth, sweet potatoes, carrots, onion, turnip, celery, barley, dried oregano (if using), ground sage (if using), and black pepper. Bring to boiling; reduce heat. Simmer, covered, for 12 to 15 minutes or until vegetables are tender. If using, stir in fresh herbs. Makes 6 servings.

Nutrition Facts per serving: 215 cal., 5 g total fat (1 g sat. fat), 30 mg chol., 717 mg sodium, 26 g carbo., 4 g fiber, 16 g pro.
Daily Values: 263% vit. A, 23% vit. C, 6% calcium, 8% iron
Exchanges: 1 Vegetable, 1½ Starch, 1½ Lean Meat

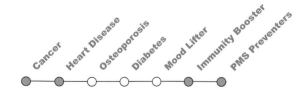

Cancer   Heart Disease   Osteoporosis   Diabetes   Mood Lifter   Immunity Booster   PMS Preventers

Caribbean-Style Pork Stew

Start to Finish: 30 minutes

Add warm summer breezes to this bean and pork stew, spiced with peppery sweet ginger and piquant cumin, and you'll think you've arrived in the islands. The soluble fiber in the black beans protects against heart disease, cancer, and diabetes, and it reduces symptoms of PMS and menopause.

1 15-ounce can black beans, rinsed and drained	1 cup chopped tomatoes
1 14½-ounce can beef broth	1 tablespoon grated fresh ginger
1¾ cups water	1 teaspoon ground cumin
12 ounces cooked lean pork, cut into bite-size strips	¼ teaspoon salt
3 plantains, peeled and cubed	¼ teaspoon crushed red pepper
½ of a 16-ounce package (2 cups) frozen pepper stir-fry	3 cups hot cooked brown rice
vegetables (yellow, green, and red sweet peppers and onion)	Fresh pineapple slices (optional)

1 In a 4-quart Dutch oven combine black beans, broth, and water. Bring to boiling. Stir in meat, plantains, frozen vegetables, tomatoes, ginger, cumin, salt, and crushed red pepper.

2 Return to boiling; reduce heat. Simmer, covered, about 10 minutes or until plantains are tender. Serve stew with rice. If desired, sprinkle with additional red pepper and garnish with pineapple slices. Makes 6 servings.

Nutrition Facts per serving: 425 cal., 9 g total fat (3 g sat. fat), 52 mg chol., 547 mg sodium, 66 g carbo., 6 g fiber, 26 g pro.
Daily Values: 22% vit. A, 77% vit. C, 4% calcium, 22% iron
Exchanges: 2½ Vegetable, 3 Starch, 1½ Lean Meat, ½ Fat

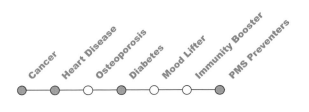

Cancer   Heart Disease   Osteoporosis   Diabetes   Mood Lifter   Immunity Booster   PMS Preventers

Sauteed Pork And Pear Salad

Start to Finish: 30 minutes

Pork and pears combine in this perfect fall salad. As with many fruits with edible skins, leaving the pears unpeeled adds color and boosts the fiber content considerably.

8	ounces boneless pork top loin roast or pork tenderloin
1/2	teaspoon black pepper
1/2	teaspoon dried sage, crushed
2	tablespoons olive oil
1/4	cup coarsely chopped hazelnuts or almonds, toasted
1/2	cup unsweetened pineapple juice
1	tablespoon honey
2	teaspoons Dijon-style mustard
1	8-ounce package torn, mixed salad greens (about 7 cups)
2	medium pears, cored and sliced

1 Trim fat from meat. Cut meat across the grain into thin bite-size strips. Sprinkle with black pepper and sage. In a large skillet heat 1 tablespoon of the oil over medium-high heat. Add meat. Cook and stir for 2 to 3 minutes or until meat is slightly pink in the center. Add nuts. Cook and stir for 30 seconds more. Remove meat mixture. Cover and keep warm.

2 For dressing, in the same skillet combine the remaining 1 tablespoon oil, the pineapple juice, honey, and mustard. Cook and stir just until bubbly, scraping up any crusty, browned bits from bottom of skillet.

3 Divide salad greens among 4 shallow bowls or dinner plates. Arrange pears on greens. Top with meat mixture and drizzle with dressing. Serve immediately. Makes 4 servings.

Nutrition Facts per serving: 282 cal., 15 g total fat (2 g sat. fat), 33 mg chol., 45 mg sodium, 24 g carbo., 4 g fiber, 14 g pro.
Daily Values: 3% vit. A, 15% vit. C, 4% calcium, 8% iron
Exchanges: 1 Vegetable, 1 Fruit, 1 1/2 Lean Meat, 2 Fat

Crockery Pork Roast With Cherries

Prep: 20 minutes **Cook:** 3½ or 7 hours

This crockery cooker recipe makes meal time more relaxing. Make your rice or noodles when you get home from work and you have a fuss-free family meal. Cherries provide ellagaic acid, which appears to counteract carcinogens in the body.

  1 **2-pound boneless pork shoulder roast or boneless pork sirloin roast**

  2 **tablespoons cooking oil**

  1 **tablespoon quick-cooking tapioca**

  1 **tablespoon snipped fresh thyme or 1 teaspoon dried thyme, crushed**

½ **teaspoon black pepper**

  1 **cup dried cherries**

  1 **medium onion, sliced**

½ **cup apple juice or apple cider**

  3 **to 4 cups hot cooked brown rice or noodles**

1 Trim fat from meat. If necessary, cut meat to fit into a 3½-, 4-, 5-, or 6-quart electric crockery cooker. In a large skillet cook meat in hot oil until evenly brown on all sides. Transfer meat to cooker.

2 Sprinkle tapioca, dried thyme (if using), and black pepper over meat. Add dried cherries and onion. Pour apple juice over all. Cover and cook on low-heat setting for 7 to 9 hours or on high-heat setting for 3½ to 4½ hours.

3 To serve, transfer meat to a serving platter. Cover and keep warm. Skim fat from cooking liquid. If using, stir fresh thyme into liquid. Serve the meat and cooking liquid with rice. Makes 8 servings.

Nutrition Facts per serving: 345 cal., 14 g total fat (5 g sat. fat), 74 mg chol., 60 mg sodium, 32 g carbo., 1 g fiber, 22 g pro.
Daily Values: 2% vit. C, 1% calcium, 14% iron
Exchanges: 1½ Fruit, 1½ Starch, 3 Medium Fat Meat, ½ Fat

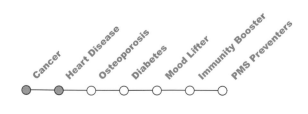

Jamaican Pork Chops With Melon Salsa

Prep: 15 minutes **Grill:** 8 minutes

Fiery chile peppers, allspice, and thyme coexist in jerk seasoning, giving a sweet and hot flavor to these grilled pork chops. Turn down the heat in the spicy seasoning with the cool mint-melon salsa that also supplies beta-carotene and vitamin C to help reduce menopause symptoms

- **1 cup chopped honeydew melon**
- **1 cup chopped cantaloupe**
- **1 tablespoon snipped fresh mint**
- **1 tablespoon honey**
- **4 boneless pork top loin chops, cut ¾ to 1 inch thick**
- **4 teaspoons Jamaican jerk seasoning**

1 For salsa, in a small bowl combine honeydew melon, cantaloupe, mint, and honey. Cover and refrigerate until ready to serve.

2 Trim fat from meat. Sprinkle Jamaican jerk seasoning evenly over meat; rub in with your fingers. Grill meat on the rack of an uncovered grill directly over medium coals for 8 to 12 minutes or until meat is slightly pink in the center and juices run clear, turning once halfway through grilling. (Or to broil place pork on the unheated rack of a broiler pan. Broil 3 to 4 inches from heat for 6 to 8 minutes, turning meat over after half of the broiling time.) Serve meat with salsa. Makes 4 servings.

Nutrition Facts per serving: 189 cal., 8 g total fat (3 g sat. fat), 51 mg chol., 231 mg sodium, 13 g carbo., 1 g fiber, 17 g pro.
Daily Values: 48% vit. C, 2% calcium, 10% iron
Exchanges: 1 Fruit, 2½ Lean Meat

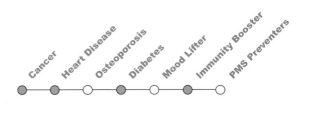

Chipotle Pork Chili

Start to Finish: 25 minutes

Robust cumin and smoky chipotle peppers jump-start the flavor in this spicy pork stew. Lean pork provides nutrients for energy production. The combination of onion, tomatoes, and garlic protects against cancer and heart disease and boosts immunity.

8 ounces lean boneless pork or boneless beef sirloin steak	1 cup water
Nonstick cooking spray	1 canned chipotle pepper in adobo sauce, chopped
1 teaspoon olive oil	1 teaspoon dried basil, crushed
1 cup chopped onion	1 teaspoon dried oregano, crushed
2 cloves garlic, minced	1 teaspoon chili powder
1 14½-ounce can low-sodium tomatoes, undrained and cut up	¼ teaspoon salt (optional)
	¼ teaspoon ground cumin
1 8-ounce can low-sodium tomato sauce	1½ cups frozen whole kernel corn

1 Trim fat from meat. Cut meat across the grain into thin bite-size strips. Lightly coat a large saucepan with cooking spray. Heat over medium-high heat. Add meat. Cook and stir for 2 to 3 minutes or until meat is brown. Remove meat.

2 Carefully pour oil into hot saucepan. Add onion and garlic; cook for 4 minutes or until onion is tender. Stir in tomatoes, tomato sauce, water, chipotle pepper, basil, oregano, chili powder, salt (if desired), and cumin. Bring to boiling; reduce heat. Simmer, covered, for 15 minutes, stirring occasionally.

3 Stir in frozen corn. Simmer, covered, for 5 minutes more, stirring occasionally. Stir in meat. Heat through. Makes 3 servings.

Nutrition Facts per serving: 355 cal., 12 g total fat (3 g sat. fat), 50 mg chol., 598 mg sodium, 43 g carbo., 4 g fiber, 23 g pro.
Daily Values: 65% vit. C, 9% calcium, 33% iron
Exchanges: 4 Vegetable, 1½ Starch, 2 Lean Meat, ½ Fat

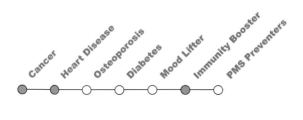

Oven-Baked Cassoulet

Prep: 20 minutes   **Bake:** 40 minutes

Our cassoulet features classic ingredients—white beans, pork, and kielbasa—but with far fewer calories and less fat than traditional versions. The white beans and veggies provide a fantastic 10 grams of fiber per serving—40 percent of the daily recommendation.

12 ounces lean boneless pork	**$\frac{2}{3}$** cup reduced-sodium chicken broth
Nonstick cooking spray	**$\frac{2}{3}$** cup water
1 teaspoon cooking oil	**2** ounces cooked turkey kielbasa, halved
1 cup chopped onion	lengthwise and sliced $\frac{1}{4}$ inch thick
1 cup chopped carrots	**1** teaspoon dried thyme, crushed
3 cloves garlic, minced	**$\frac{1}{4}$** teaspoon dried rosemary, crushed
2 15-ounce cans white kidney (cannellini) beans,	**$\frac{1}{4}$** teaspoon black pepper
rinsed and drained	**2** tablespoons snipped fresh parsley
4 plum tomatoes, chopped	

1 Trim fat from meat. Cut meat into $\frac{1}{2}$-inch pieces. Lightly coat a 4-quart oven-going Dutch oven with cooking spray. Heat over medium-high heat. Add meat. Cook about 4 minutes or until meat is brown. Remove meat.

2 Carefully pour oil into hot Dutch oven. Add onion, carrots, and garlic; cook until onion is tender. Stir in meat, beans, tomatoes, broth, water, kielbasa, thyme, rosemary, and black pepper.

3 Bake, covered, in a 325° oven for 40 to 45 minutes or until meat and carrots are tender. Sprinkle each serving with parsley. Makes 5 servings.

Nutrition Facts per serving: 243 cal., 7 g total fat (2 g sat. fat), 38 mg chol., 497 mg sodium, 32 g carbo., 10 g fiber, 23 g pro.
Daily Values: 26% vit. C, 5% calcium, 21% iron
Exchanges: 2 Vegetable, 1 Starch, 2$\frac{1}{2}$ Lean Meat

Range-Top Cassoulet: Prepare Oven-Baked Cassoulet as directed, except instead of baking, simmer, covered, about 15 minutes or until the meat and carrots are tender.

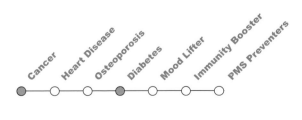

ChickenTurkey

Grilled Chicken and Rice Salad, page 92

Grilled Chicken And Rice Salad   **Prep:** 20 minutes   **Grill:** 12 minutes

Antioxidant-loaded artichokes combine with cruciferous cabbage and carotenoid-rich carrots in this thyme-scented salad. These crusaders fight against cancer, heart disease, and diabetes. (Pictured on page 91.)

1	recipe Thyme Vinaigrette
12	ounces skinless, boneless chicken breast halves or thighs
1	cup loose-pack frozen French-cut green beans
2	cups cooked brown rice and wild rice blend, chilled
1	14-ounce can artichoke hearts, drained and quartered
1	cup shredded red cabbage
½	cup shredded carrot
1	green onion, sliced
	Lettuce leaves (optional)

1 Prepare Thyme Vinaigrette. Brush chicken with 2 tablespoons of the vinaigrette; set aside the remaining vinaigrette until ready to serve.

2 Grill chicken on the rack of an uncovered grill directly over medium coals for 12 to 15 minutes or until chicken is tender and no longer pink, turning once halfway through grilling. (Or broil on the unheated rack of a broiler pan 4 to 5 inches from the heat for 12 to 15 minutes, turning once halfway through broiling.) Cut chicken into bite-size strips.

3 Meanwhile, rinse green beans with cool water for 30 seconds; drain well. In a large bowl toss together beans, cooked rice, artichoke hearts, cabbage, carrot, and green onion. Pour the remaining vinaigrette over rice mixture; toss to gently coat.

4 If desired, arrange lettuce leaves on 4 dinner plates. Top with the rice mixture and chicken. Makes 4 servings.

Thyme Vinaigrette: In a screw-top jar combine ¼ cup white wine vinegar; 2 tablespoons olive oil; 2 tablespoons water; 1 tablespoon grated Parmesan cheese; 2 teaspoons snipped fresh thyme; 1 clove garlic, minced; ¼ teaspoon salt; and ¼ teaspoon black pepper. Cover and shake well.

Nutrition Facts per serving: 305 cal., 8 g total fat (1 g sat. fat), 50 mg chol., 541 mg sodium, 29 g carbo., 6 g fiber, 26 g pro.
Daily Values: 92% vit. A, 27% vit. C, 9% calcium, 20% iron
Exchanges: 1 Vegetable, 1½ Starch, 3 Very Lean Meat, 1 Fat

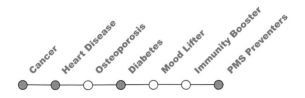

Broiled Pineapple Chicken Salad

Prep: 20 minutes   **Broil:** 12 minutes

Fresh pineapple, refreshing jicama, and sweet carrot highlight this summer-fresh chicken salad. Vitamin C-loaded pineapple protects against heart disease, cancer, diabetes, and arthritis. It also enhances the immune system. Vitamin A-packed carrots assist in the fight against cancer and boost the immune system.

4   medium skinless, boneless chicken breast halves or
     turkey breast tenderloin steaks (about 1 pound total)

1/4   of a medium pineapple, cored and cut into wedges

6   cups shredded lettuce

1   cup peeled jicama cut into thin bite-size strips

1   cup coarsely shredded carrots

1   6-ounce carton tropical or pineapple fat-free yogurt

2   tablespoons pineapple or orange juice

1/2   teaspoon curry powder

1/8   teaspoon black pepper

1 Place chicken on the unheated rack of a broiler pan. Broil 4 to 5 inches from the heat for 6 minutes. Turn chicken. Add pineapple wedges to broiler pan. Broil for 6 to 9 minutes more or until chicken is tender and no longer pink, turning pineapple once during broiling. Cut chicken into bite-size strips.

2 Arrange shredded lettuce on 4 dinner plates. Top with chicken and pineapple. Sprinkle with jicama and carrots.

3 For dressing, in a small bowl stir together yogurt, pineapple juice, curry powder, and black pepper. Drizzle over salads. Makes 4 servings.

Nutrition Facts per serving: 221 cal., 4 g total fat (1 g sat. fat), 61 mg chol., 95 mg sodium, 21 g carbo., 2 g fiber, 25 g pro.
Daily Values: 80% vit. A, 31% vit. C, 8% calcium, 12% iron
Exchanges: 2 Vegetable, 1 Fruit, 3 Very Lean Meat

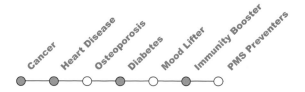

Chicken In Shiitake Mushroom Sauce

Prep: 20 minutes **Cook:** 40 minutes

The aromatic flavors of parsley, thyme, and rosemary are sure to wow family and friends. Chunky carrots and tiny pearl onions combine with a vermouth-scented sauce, providing enhanced immunity, anticancer benefits, heart protection, blood sugar control, and healthier skin.

3 **pounds meaty chicken pieces (breasts, thighs, and drumsticks)**	¼ **cup dry vermouth**
Salt	1 **14½-ounce can chicken broth**
Black pepper	3 **tablespoons snipped fresh parsley**
2 **tablespoons olive oil**	1 **tablespoon snipped fresh thyme**
8 **ounces pearl onions**	1 **tablespoon snipped fresh rosemary**
4 **medium carrots, cut into 1-inch pieces**	8 **ounces fresh shiitake mushrooms, halved**
	Fresh rosemary sprigs (optional)

1 Skin chicken. Sprinkle chicken with salt and black pepper. In a 12-inch skillet heat oil over medium heat. Add chicken. Cook about 10 minutes or until chicken is golden brown, turning to brown evenly. Remove chicken.

2 Add pearl onions and carrots to skillet. Cook about 5 minutes or until onions are golden brown, stirring occasionally. Add vermouth, scraping up any crusty browned bits from bottom of skillet. Return chicken to skillet. Pour broth over chicken; sprinkle with parsley, thyme, and rosemary.

3 Bring to boiling; reduce heat. Simmer, covered, about 40 minutes or until chicken is tender and no longer pink, adding mushrooms the last 10 minutes of cooking. If desired, garnish with additional fresh rosemary. Makes 4 to 6 servings.

Nutrition Facts per serving: 446 cal., 20 g total fat (4 g sat. fat), 138 mg chol., 624 mg sodium, 14 g carbo., 4 g fiber, 50 g pro.
Daily Values: 311% vit. A, 20% vit. C, 6% calcium, 18% iron
Exchanges: 3 Vegetable, 6 Lean Meat, 1 Fat

Cancer Heart Disease Osteoporosis Diabetes Mood Lifter Immunity Booster PMS Preventers

Ginger-Spiced Chicken

Prep: 15 minutes **Marinate:** 2 hours **Bake:** 20 minutes

Coriander, cinnamon, ginger, and paprika give chicken breasts marinated in orange juice a hint of North African flavor. The low-fat chicken is a great protein source to fight heart disease and diabetes, and ginger and garlic help lift moods.

4 medium skinless, boneless chicken breast halves (about 1 pound total)	1 teaspoon ground corinader
4 green onions, finely chopped	1/2 teaspoon paprika
1/2 cup orange juice	1/4 teaspoon salt
1 tablespoon brown sugar	1/4 teaspoon ground cinnamon
1 tablespoon finely chopped fresh ginger	1/4 teaspoon black pepper
1 tablespoon olive oil	Nonstick cooking spray
2 cloves garlic, minced	2 cups hot cooked basmati or long grain rice

1 Place chicken in a plastic bag set in a shallow dish. For marinade, in a small bowl combine green onions, orange juice, brown sugar, ginger, oil, garlic, coriander, paprika, salt, cinnamon, and black pepper. Pour over chicken; seal bag. Marinate in the refrigerator for 2 to 6 hours, turning bag occasionally. Drain chicken, reserving marinade.

2 Lightly coat a 2-quart rectangular baking dish with cooking spray. Arrange chicken in the prepared baking dish; pour marinade over chicken.

3 Bake, uncovered, in a 375° oven about 20 minutes or until chicken is tender and no longer pink. Transfer chicken to a serving platter. Strain the juices remaining in baking dish; stir juices into rice. Serve the chicken with rice. Makes 4 servings.

Nutrition Facts per serving: 290 cal., 5 g total fat (1 g sat. fat), 66 mg chol., 209 mg sodium, 30 g carbo., 1 g fiber, 29 g pro.
Daily Values: 6% vit. A, 33% vit. C, 4% calcium, 12% iron
Exchanges: 1/2 Fruit, 1 1/2 Starch, 3 1/2 Very Lean Meat

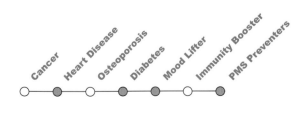

Basque Chicken   **Prep:** 25 minutes **Cook:** 10 minutes

Piquant garlic, red pepper, and oregano create a pleasing, saucy fusion with tomatoes, sweet peppers, and onion. The scrumptious vegetable and garlic combination fights cancer, protects against heart disease, lowers cholesterol, boosts immunity, and helps control blood sugars.

2 tablespoons all-purpose flour	1 teaspoon paprika
4 medium skinless, boneless chicken breast halves	1/8 teaspoon ground red pepper
(about 1 pound total)	1 14 1/2-ounce can diced tomatoes, undrained
1 tablespoon olive oil	1/4 cup reduced-sodium chicken broth
2 large green and/or yellow sweet peppers, cut into	1/4 cup sliced, pitted ripe olives
bite-size strips	1 tablespoon snipped fresh oregano
1 large onion, halved lengthwise and thinly sliced	Hot cooked bulgur or barley pilaf (optional)
3 cloves garlic, minced	

1 Place flour in a shallow dish. Dip chicken in flour to coat. In a large skillet heat oil over medium-high heat. Add chicken. Cook about 4 minutes or until chicken is brown, turning once. Remove chicken.

2 Add sweet peppers, onion, and garlic to skillet. Cook and stir for 3 to 4 minutes or until vegetables are nearly tender. Add paprika and ground red pepper. Cook and stir for 1 minute more.

3 Stir in tomatoes, broth, and olives. Bring to boiling. Return chicken to skillet, spooning tomato mixture over chicken. Reduce heat. Simmer, covered, about 10 minutes or until chicken is tender and no longer pink.

4 Transfer chicken to a serving platter. Stir oregano into tomato mixture. Spoon the tomato mixture over chicken. If desired, serve with bulgur pilaf. Makes 4 servings.

Nutrition Facts per serving: 241 cal., 6 g total fat (1 g sat. fat), 66 mg chol., 343 mg sodium, 17 g carbo., 3 g fiber, 29 g pro.
Daily Values: 15% vit. A, 104% vit. C, 8% calcium, 12% iron
Exchanges: 2 Vegetable, 1/2 Starch, 3 1/2 Very Lean Meat, 1/2 Fat

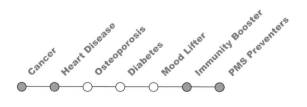

Chicken Paella

Prep: 20 minutes   **Cook:** 10 minutes   **Stand:** 5 minutes

Red sweet pepper brightens this spiced chicken, making this one-dish meal the perfect family dinner. Its health benefits include enhancing moods, boosting immunity, reducing the pain of arthritis, and preventing cancer, diabetes, and heart disease.

2 tablespoons olive oil	1¾ cups instant brown rice
1 cup chopped onion	1 14½-ounce can reduced-sodium chicken broth
1 large red sweet pepper, cut into thin strips	¼ cup water
12 ounces skinless, boneless chicken breast halves, cut into bite-size strips	¼ teaspoon salt
1 clove garlic, minced	¼ teaspoon black pepper
½ teaspoon paprika	2 medium tomatoes, seeded and chopped
¼ teaspoon ground turmeric	1 cup frozen peas

1 In a large skillet heat oil over medium heat. Add the onion and sweet pepper; cook and stir about 4 minutes or until the onion is tender.

2 Add chicken, garlic, paprika, and turmeric. Cook and stir until chicken is brown. Stir in uncooked rice, broth, water, salt, and black pepper.

3 Bring to boiling; reduce heat. Simmer, covered, for 10 minutes. Remove from heat. Stir in tomatoes and peas. Cover and let stand for 5 minutes before serving. Makes 4 servings.

Nutrition Facts per serving: 333 cal., 9 g total fat (1 g sat. fat), 49 mg chol., 506 mg sodium, 37 g carbo., 6 g fiber, 27 g pro.
Daily Values: 74% vit. A, 176% vit. C, 3% calcium, 9% iron
Exchanges: 1 Vegetable, 2 Starch, 2½ Lean Meat

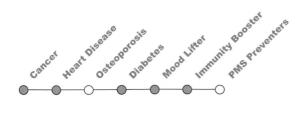

Tex-Mex Chicken Tacos

Prep: 20 minutes **Marinate:** 1 hour **Cook:** 15 minutes

The citrus fruits featured in this tangy marinade protect against cancer and heart disease because they're brimming with vitamin C and plant compounds. An orange contains more than 170 different phytochemicals.

12	ounces skinless, boneless chicken breast halves, cut into bite-size strips	$1/8$	teaspoon salt
$1/2$	cup orange juice	$1/8$	teaspoon black pepper
$1/4$	cup snipped fresh cilantro	2	teaspoons cooking oil
1	teaspoon finely shredded lime peel	1	medium red sweet pepper, cut into thin strips
2	tablespoons lime juice	1	cup frozen whole kernel corn
1	fresh jalapeño pepper, seeded and finely chopped*	$1^1/2$	teaspoons cornstarch
3	cloves garlic, minced	8	6-inch corn tortillas
		$1/2$	cup light dairy sour cream

1 Place chicken in a plastic bag set in a shallow dish. For marinade, in a small bowl combine orange juice, cilantro, lime peel, lime juice, jalapeño pepper, garlic, salt, and black pepper. Pour over chicken; seal bag. Marinate in the refrigerator for 1 to 2 hours, turning bag occasionally.

2 Drain chicken, reserving marinade. In a large nonstick skillet heat oil over medium-high heat. Add sweet pepper strips; cook and stir until crisp-tender. Remove sweet pepper strips.

3 Add chicken to skillet. Cook and stir for 3 to 4 minutes or until chicken is tender and no longer pink. Stir in corn; heat through. Combine the marinade and cornstarch; add to chicken mixture. Cook and stir until thickened and bubbly. Cook and stir for 2 minutes more. Return sweet pepper strips to skillet; stir to combine.

4 Wrap tortillas in microwave-safe paper towels. Microwave on 100% power (high) for 45 to 60 seconds or until warm. Divide the chicken mixture among tortillas and top with sour cream. Fold the tortillas over chicken mixture. Makes 4 servings.

Nutrition Facts per serving: 362 cal., 9 g total fat (3 g sat. fat), 61 mg chol., 138 mg sodium, 47 g carbo., 4 g fiber, 26 g pro.
Daily Values: 42% vit. A, 123% vit. C, 11% calcium, 22% iron
Exchanges: $1/2$ Vegetable, $1/2$ Fruit, $2^1/2$ Starch, $2^1/2$ Very Lean Meat, 1 Fat

*Note: Hot peppers contain volatile oils in the seeds and inner membranes that can burn eyes, lips, and sensitive skin. Wear plastic gloves when handling hot peppers and wash your hands thoroughly with soap and water afterwards.

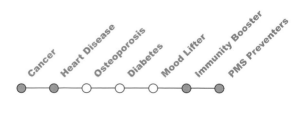

Kale, Lentil, and Chicken Soup, page 102

Mediterranean Chicken and Pasta, page 103

Kale, Lentil, And Chicken Soup   **Prep:** 25 minutes   **Cook:** 30 minutes

Chicken soup is made even better by adding kale, lentils, and tomato. This home-style soup is packed with flavor and nutrients (e.g., antioxidants, flavonoids, selenium, carotenoids, and calcium), which supply many health advantages. Kale, a member of the cruciferous family, packs cancer-fighting potential. (Pictured on page 100.)

1 tablespoon olive oil	4 cups coarsely chopped kale (about 8 ounces)
1 cup chopped onion	½ teaspoon salt
1 cup coarsely chopped carrots	⅛ teaspoon black pepper
2 cloves garlic, minced	1½ cups cubed cooked chicken
6 cups reduced-sodium chicken broth	1 medium tomato, seeded and chopped
1 tablespoon snipped fresh basil or	½ cup dry red lentils
1 teaspoon dried basil, crushed	

1 In a large saucepan heat oil over medium-low heat. Add onion, carrots, and garlic. Cook, covered, for 5 to 7 minutes or until vegetables are nearly tender, stirring occasionally.

2 Add broth and, if using, dried basil to vegetable mixture. Bring to boiling; reduce heat. Simmer, covered, for 10 minutes. Stir in kale, salt, and black pepper. Return to boiling; reduce heat. Simmer, covered, for 10 minutes.

3 Stir in chicken, tomato, lentils, and, if using, fresh basil. Simmer, covered, for 5 to 10 minutes more or until kale and lentils are tender. Makes 6 servings.

Nutrition Facts per serving: 199 cal., 5 g total fat (1 g sat. fat), 31 mg chol., 871 mg sodium, 20 g carbo., 7 g fiber, 20 g pro.
Daily Values: 170% vit. A, 59% vit. C, 8% calcium, 15% iron
Exchanges: 2 Vegetable, ½ Starch, 2 Very Lean Meat, ½ Fat

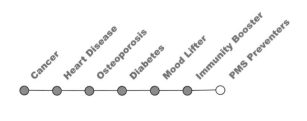

Cancer   Heart Disease   Osteoporosis   Diabetes   Mood Lifter   Immunity Booster   PMS Preventers

Mediterranean Chicken And Pasta   **Start to finish:** 30 minutes

This colorful, heart-healthy dish contains only 1 gram of saturated fat per serving. The artichokes provide a plant compound called silymarin, a potent antioxidant linked to cancer prevention. (Pictured on 7 and 102.)

1	**6-ounce jar marinated artichoke hearts**
1	**tablespoon olive oil**
12	**ounces skinless, boneless chicken breast halves, cut into ³/₄-inch cubes**
3	**cloves garlic, thinly sliced**
¹/₄	**cup chicken broth**
¹/₄	**cup dry white wine**
1	**tablespoon small fresh oregano leaves or 1 teaspoon dried oregano, crushed**
1	**7-ounce jar roasted red sweet peppers, drained and cut into strips**
¹/₄	**cup pitted kalamata olives**
3	**cups hot cooked campanelle or penne pasta**
¹/₄	**cup crumbled feta cheese (optional)**

1 Drain artichokes, reserving marinade. Set aside. In a large skillet heat oil over medium-high heat. Add chicken and garlic. Cook and stir until chicken is brown. Add the reserved artichoke marinade, broth, wine, and, if using, dried oregano.

2 Bring to boiling; reduce heat. Simmer, covered, for 10 minutes. Stir in artichokes, roasted peppers, olives, and, if using, fresh oregano. Heat through.

3 To serve, spoon the chicken mixture over pasta. If desired, sprinkle with feta cheese. Makes 4 servings.

Nutrition Facts per serving: 337 cal., 9 g total fat (1 g sat. fat), 49 mg chol., 323 mg sodium, 36 g carbo., 2 g fiber, 26 g pro.
Daily Values: 1% vit. A, 104% vit. C, 4% calcium, 15% iron
Exchanges: 1 ¹/₂ Starch, 3 Lean Meat

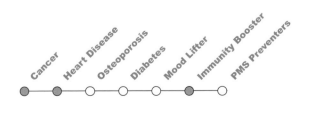

Chicken With Chunky Vegetable Sauce   **Prep:** 15 minutes   **Cook:** 25 minutes

Count on this Mediterranean-inspired chicken entrée for great nutrition and flavor. Juicy diced tomatoes mingle with oregano and artichoke hearts to provide great taste as well as cancer protection, increased immunity, and blood sugar control.

2 **tablespoons all-purpose flour**	$^1/_3$ **cup reduced-sodium chicken broth**
4 **medium skinless, boneless chicken breast halves**	1 **tablespoon snipped fresh oregano or 1 teaspoon dried**
(about 1 pound total)	**oregano, crushed**
1 **cup finely chopped onion**	**Dash black pepper**
1 **tablespoon olive oil**	2 **teaspoons drained capers or 2 tablespoons chopped, pitted**
2 **cloves garlic, minced**	**ripe olives**
1 **14$^1/_2$-ounce can diced tomatoes, undrained**	2 **cups hot cooked rice**
1 **14-ounce can artichoke hearts, drained and halved**	**Kalamata olives or pitted ripe olives (optional)**

1 Place flour in a shallow dish. Dip chicken in flour to coat. Set aside.

2 In a large skillet cook onion in hot oil over medium heat for 3 minutes. Stir in garlic; push onion mixture to sides of skillet. Add chicken. Cook about 4 minutes or until chicken is brown, turning once. Add tomatoes, artichoke hearts, broth, dried oregano (if using), and pepper; stir just to combine.

3 Bring to boiling; reduce heat. Simmer, covered, about 10 minutes or until chicken is tender and no longer pink. Remove chicken; cover and keep warm.

4 Simmer tomato mixture, uncovered, about 3 minutes or until reduced to desired consistency. Stir in capers and, if using, fresh oregano. Serve the chicken over rice. Top with the tomato mixture. If desired, garnish with ripe olives. Makes 4 servings.

Nutrition Facts per serving: 341 cal., 6 g total fat (1 g sat. fat), 66 mg chol., 635 mg sodium, 36 g carbo., 5 g fiber, 33 g pro.
Daily Values: 4% vit. A, 31% vit. C, 11% calcium, 26% iron
Exchanges: 2$^1/_2$ Vegetable, 1$^1/_2$ Starch, 3$^1/_2$ Very Lean Meat

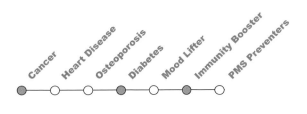

Chicken Stir-Fry With Sesame Tofu   **Start to Finish:** 25 minutes

Chicken strips and tofu—cooked in savory Asian flavors of sesame, oyster sauce, and ginger—turn a simple stir-fry into a satisfying meal. This chicken, tofu, and veggie combination offers protection from cancer, heart disease, and diabetes.

1 12- to 16-ounce package firm tub-style tofu (fresh bean curd), drained and cut into $^{3}/_{4}$-inch cubes	1 tablespoon grated fresh ginger
$^{1}/_{3}$ cup reduced-sodium chicken broth	2 cloves garlic, minced
2 tablespoons oyster sauce	8 ounces skinless, boneless chicken thighs, cut into bite-size strips
2 tablespoons reduced-sodium soy sauce	2 cups broccoli florets
1 teaspoon toasted sesame oil	1 medium red sweet pepper, cut into thin strips
2 teaspoons cornstarch	3 green onions, cut into $^{1}/_{2}$-inch pieces
2 teaspoons peanut oil	3 cups hot cooked jasmine rice or long grain rice

1 Place tofu in a medium bowl. In a small bowl stir together the broth, oyster sauce, soy sauce, and sesame oil. Drizzle 2 tablespoons of the soy sauce mixture over tofu; toss gently to coat. For sauce, stir cornstarch into the remaining soy sauce mixture. Set aside.

2 Pour peanut oil into a wok or large nonstick skillet. Heat wok over medium-high heat. Stir-fry ginger and garlic in hot oil for 30 seconds. Add chicken. Stir-fry for 3 to 4 minutes or until chicken is tender and no longer pink. Remove from wok.

3 Add broccoli, sweet pepper, and green onions to hot wok. Stir-fry about 3 minutes or until vegetables are crisp-tender. Return chicken to wok. Stir sauce; add to chicken mixture. Cook and stir until thickened and bubbly.

4 Drain tofu; add to chicken mixture. Cook and stir gently about 1 minute or until heated through. Serve immediately over rice. Makes 4 to 6 servings.

Nutrition Facts per serving: 369 cal., 10 g total fat (2 g sat. fat), 45 mg chol., 678 mg sodium, 44 g carbo., 3 g fiber, 26 g pro.
Daily Values: 45% vit. A, 141% vit. C, 18% calcium, 22% iron
Exchanges: 1 Vegetable, 2½ Starch, 2½ Lean Meat

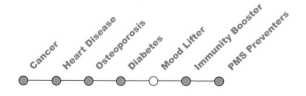

Chicken With Broccoli And Garlic   **Start to Finish:** 35 minutes

Garlic is an amazing food. Those tiny cloves possess loads of flavor and fight cancer, arthritis, and heart disease. Add the antioxidants of broccoli in this dish for more cancer- and heart disease-fighting power.

- ¼ **cup all-purpose flour**
- ½ **teaspoon salt**
- ¼ **teaspoon black pepper**
- 4 **medium skinless, boneless chicken thighs (about 12 ounces total)**
- 1 **tablespoon olive oil**
- 1 **bulb garlic, separated into cloves and sliced (about ¼ cup)**
- 1 **cup chicken broth**
- 3 **tablespoons red wine vinegar**
- 1 **to 2 tablespoons honey**
- 6 **cups packaged shredded broccoli (broccoli slaw mix)**
- 2 **tablespoons chopped pecans, toasted**

1 In a plastic bag combine flour, salt, and pepper. Add chicken, shaking to coat.

2 In a large skillet cook chicken in hot oil over medium heat for 12 to 15 minutes or until chicken is tender and no longer pink, turning once. Transfer chicken to a serving platter; cover and keep warm.

3 Add garlic to skillet. Cook and stir for 1 minute. Add broth, vinegar, and honey. Bring to boiling; reduce heat. Simmer, uncovered, for 5 minutes. Stir in broccoli. Return to boiling; reduce heat. Simmer, covered, for 5 to 8 minutes more or until broccoli is tender. Stir in pecans. Spoon the broccoli mixture over chicken. Makes 4 servings.

Nutrition Facts per serving: 234 cal., 9 g total fat (2 g sat. fat), 57 mg chol., 625 mg sodium, 20 g carbo., 5 g fiber, 20 g pro.
Daily Values: 39% vit. A, 181% vit. C, 9% calcium, 14% iron
Exchanges: 2 Vegetable, ½ Starch, 2 Lean Meat, ½ Fat

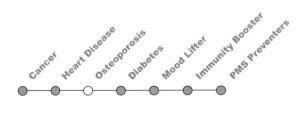

Vegetable-Stuffed Chicken

Start to Finish: 35 minutes

The Gruyère cheese in this chicken dish adds a nutty richness. It also provides conjugated linoleic acid, a type of polyunsaturated fat that may fight heart disease, cancer, and diabetes. The mushrooms contribute compounds believed to help prevent blood clots and cancer.

Nonstick cooking spray	1½ ounces Gruyère cheese, cut into 4 slices
1½ cups chopped fresh mushrooms	1 teaspoon olive oil
1 clove garlic, minced	⅔ cup reduced-sodium chicken broth
2 tablespoons chopped roasted red sweet pepper	⅓ cup Madeira or reduced-sodium chicken broth
¼ teaspoon dried marjoram, crushed	1 tablespoon cold water
4 medium skinless, boneless chicken breast halves (about 1 pound total)	2 teaspoons cornstarch
	1 tablespoon snipped fresh parsley

1 For stuffing, spray a medium nonstick skillet with cooking spray. Heat skillet over medium heat. Add mushrooms and garlic; cook until mushrooms are tender, stirring occasionally. Stir in roasted sweet pepper and marjoram.

2 Cut a horizontal slit in the thickest part of each chicken piece, forming a pocket. Divide the cheese and stuffing among the pockets. Secure with wooden toothpicks.

3 In a large skillet cook chicken in hot oil over medium heat about 4 minutes or until brown, turning once. Pour broth and Madeira over chicken. Bring to boiling; reduce heat. Simmer, uncovered, about 10 minutes or until chicken is tender and no longer pink. Remove chicken.

4 Strain the juices remaining in skillet; measure juices and return to skillet. If necessary, boil gently, uncovered, until liquid is reduced to about ¾ cup. In a small bowl combine the water and cornstarch; stir into the liquid in skillet. Cook and stir until thickened and bubbly. Return chicken to skillet; cook for 2 minutes more. Remove toothpicks from chicken. Sprinkle with parsley. Makes 4 servings.

Nutrition Facts per serving: 208 cal., 8 g total fat (3 g sat. fat), 71 mg chol., 199 mg sodium, 4 g carbo., 1 g fiber, 26 g pro.
Daily Values: 25% vit. C, 10% calcium, 9% iron
Exchanges: ½ Vegetable, 3½ Lean Meat

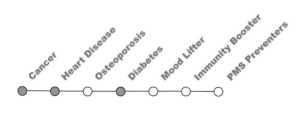

Chicken With Apples And Sage   **Start to Finish:** 30 minutes

The classic flavor combination of sweet fall apples and fragrant sage graces chicken breasts in this low-fat entrée. Sweet peppers in the savory sauce work with apples to defend against cancer, reduce heart disease, increase immunity, protect against diabetes, and reduce the effects of arthritis.

Nonstick cooking spray	1$\frac{1}{2}$ **teaspoons snipped fresh sage or $\frac{1}{2}$ teaspoon**
4 **medium skinless, boneless chicken**	**dried sage, crushed**
breast halves (about 1 pound total)	1 **clove garlic, minced**
$\frac{1}{8}$ **teaspoon salt**	$\frac{1}{4}$ **teaspoon black pepper**
1 **cup apple juice or apple cider**	1 **tablespoon cornstarch**
1 **medium red or green sweet pepper, cut**	1 **tablespoon cold water**
into 1-inch pieces	2 **medium red and/or green cooking apples,**
$\frac{1}{4}$ **cup chopped onion**	**thinly sliced**

1 Coat a large skillet with cooking spray. Heat skillet over medium-high heat. Sprinkle chicken with salt. Place chicken in skillet. Cook for 8 to 10 minutes or until chicken is tender and no longer pink, turning once. Remove chicken.

2 Add apple juice, sweet pepper, onion, dried sage (if using), garlic, and black pepper to skillet. Bring to boiling; reduce heat. Simmer, covered, for 2 minutes.

3 In a small bowl combine cornstarch and water; stir into juice mixture. Stir in apples. Cook and stir until thickened and bubbly. Cook and stir for 2 minutes more. If using, stir in fresh sage. Return chicken to skillet; heat through. Makes 4 servings.

Nutrition Facts per serving: 203 cal., 4 g total fat (1 g sat. fat), 59 mg chol., 123 mg sodium, 21 g carbo., 2 g fiber, 22 g pro.
Daily Values: 60% vit. C, 2% calcium, 8% iron
Exchanges: 1$\frac{1}{2}$ Fruit, 3$\frac{1}{2}$ Very Lean Meat

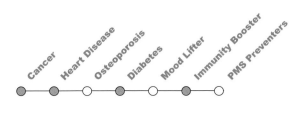

Bangkok Stir-Fry, page 112

Grilled Greek-Style Turkey Burgers, page 113

Bangkok Stir-Fry   **Start to Finish:** 25 minutes

Hot jalapeño peppers add more than verve to this pungent stir-fry. Vitamin C, lutein, and zeaxanthin from the peppers team with a healthy dose of vitamin C from the pineapple to fight cancer and arthritis. Niacin, abundant in chicken, has also been shown to help normal cells resist turning cancerous. (Pictured on page 111.)

2 tablespoons fish sauce (nam pla)	$\frac{1}{4}$ of a pineapple, peeled, cored, and cut into $\frac{1}{4}$-inch wedges
1 tablespoon lime juice	1 small cucumber, cut into thin bite-size strips (about 1 cup)
2 teaspoons minced fresh lemongrass or	1 or 2 fresh jalapeño peppers, seeded and finely chopped*
1 teaspoon finely shredded lemon peel	12 ounces skinless, boneless chicken breast halves, cut into
4 teaspoons cooking oil	thin bite-size strips
1 large red onion, halved lengthwise and sliced	3 cups hot cooked aromatic rice (such as jasmine or basmati)
3 cloves garlic, minced	Snipped fresh cilantro or parsley (optional)

1 For sauce, in a small bowl stir together fish sauce, lime juice, and lemongrass; set aside.

2 Pour 2 teaspoons of the oil into a wok or large skillet. Heat wok over medium-high heat. Stir-fry onion and garlic in hot oil for 2 minutes. Add pineapple, cucumber, and jalapeño peppers. Stir-fry for 2 minutes more. Remove from wok.

3 Add the remaining 2 teaspoons oil to hot wok. Add chicken. Stir-fry for 2 to 3 minutes or until chicken is tender and no longer pink. Return onion mixture to wok. Add sauce. Cook and stir about 1 minute or until heated through. Serve immediately over rice. If desired, sprinkle with snipped parsley. Makes 4 servings.

Nutrition Facts per serving: 343 cal., 7 g total fat (1 g sat. fat), 49 mg chol., 510 mg sodium, 45 g carbo., 2 g fiber, 24 g pro.
Daily Values: 2% vit. A, 25% vit. C, 7% calcium, 15% iron
Exchanges: 1 Fruit, 2 Starch, 3 Very Lean Meat, ½ Fat

---

*Note: Hot peppers contain volatile oils in the seeds and inner membranes that can burn eyes, lips, and sensitive skin. Wear plastic gloves when handling hot peppers and wash your hands thoroughly with soap and water afterwards.

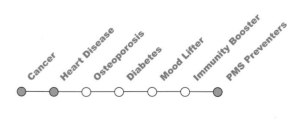

Grilled Greek-Style Turkey Burgers

Prep: 20 minutes **Grill:** 14 minutes

These burgers, aside from being a tasty alternative to beef, also supply folic acid, which is necessary to protect against heart disease and some types of cancer. Turkey also offers a low-fat meat choice for those who want to lower their cholesterol levels. (Pictured on page 110.)

$\frac{1}{3}$ **cup fine dry wheat bread crumbs**

1 **slightly beaten egg white**

1 **tablespoon milk**

1 **0.7-ounce envelope Italian salad dressing mix (5 teaspoons)**

1 **pound lean uncooked ground turkey or chicken**

4 **pita bread rounds, toasted, or 4 whole wheat hamburger buns, split and toasted**

1 **recipe Greek Salsa**

$\frac{1}{4}$ **cup crumbled feta cheese**

1 In a medium bowl combine bread crumbs, egg white, milk, and half of the salad dressing mix. Add turkey; mix well. (Reserve the remaining half of salad dressing mix for Greek Salsa.) Shape turkey mixture into four $\frac{3}{4}$-inch-thick patties.

2 Grill patties on the rack of an uncovered grill directly over medium coals for 14 to 18 minutes or until turkey is done (165°), turning once halfway through grilling. (Or broil on the unheated rack of a broiler pan 4 to 5 inches from the heat for 10 to 12 minutes, turning once halfway through broiling.)

3 Serve the burgers on pita bread rounds. Top with Greek Salsa and sprinkle with feta cheese. Makes 4 servings.

Greek Salsa: In a small bowl stir together 2 tablespoons white wine vinegar, 2 teaspoons olive oil, and the remaining half of the salad dressing mix. Stir in 1 cup finely chopped tomato, $\frac{1}{4}$ cup finely chopped cucumber, and $\frac{1}{4}$ cup finely chopped, pitted kalamata or ripe olives. Makes about $1\frac{1}{3}$ cups.

Nutrition Facts per serving: 403 cal., 18 g total fat (5 g sat. fat), 96 mg chol., 1,177 mg sodium, 32 g carbo., 3 g fiber, 28 g pro.
Daily Values: 7% vit. A, 15% vit. C, 10% calcium, 20% iron
Exchanges: 2 Starch, 3 Medium Fat Meat, $\frac{1}{2}$ Fat

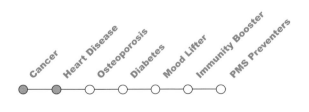

Turkey And Peppers

Start to Finish: 25 minutes

Low-fat turkey cutlets get a colorful treatment from sweet and hot peppers. Both types of peppers contain vitamin C and beta-carotene. Jalapeños get their heat from capsaicin, a phytochemical with antibacterial and anticancer properties.

4   ¼- to ⅜-inch-thick turkey breast slices (about 12 ounces total)

    Salt

    Black pepper

1   tablespoon olive oil

2   medium red, green, and/or yellow sweet peppers, cut into thin strips

1   medium onion, halved lengthwise and sliced

1   fresh jalapeño pepper, seeded and thinly sliced*

¾   cup chicken broth

1   tablespoon all-purpose flour

1   teaspoon paprika

    Hot cooked brown rice (optional)

1 Sprinkle turkey lightly with salt and black pepper. In a large nonstick skillet cook turkey in hot oil over medium-high heat for 4 to 5 minutes or until turkey is tender and no longer pink, turning once. (If necessary, reduce heat to medium to prevent overbrowning.) Transfer turkey to a serving platter; cover and keep warm.

2 Add the sweet peppers, onion, and jalapeño pepper to skillet. Cook, covered, for 4 to 5 minutes or until vegetables are crisp-tender, stirring occasionally.

3 In a screw-top jar combine broth, flour, and paprika; shake well. Add to pepper mixture. Cook and stir over medium heat until thickened and bubbly. Cook and stir for 1 minute more. Spoon the pepper mixture over turkey. If desired, serve with rice. Makes 4 servings.

Nutrition Facts per serving: 164 cal., 4 g total fat (1 g sat. fat), 53 mg chol., 324 mg sodium, 8 g carbo., 2 g fiber, 23 g pro.
Daily Values: 67% vit. A, 157% vit. C, 2% calcium, 9% iron
Exchanges: 1 Vegetable, 3 Very Lean Meat, ½ Fat

---

*Note: Hot peppers contain volatile oils in the seeds and inner membranes that can burn eyes, lips, and sensitive skin. Wear plastic gloves when handling hot peppers and wash your hands thoroughly with soap and water afterwards.

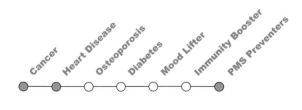

Turkey And Cranberry Sandwiches

Start to Finish: 15 minutes

Though not apparent from looks alone, pungent and peppery watercress is a cruciferous vegetable like broccoli, cauliflower, and Brussels sprouts. Watercress offers a wealth of phytochemicals that protect against cancer.

- **8 slices artisan-style walnut bread or wheat bread**
- **12 ounces thinly sliced turkey breast or smoked turkey breast**
- **1/2 cup watercress leaves or 4 romaine lettuce leaves**
- **1/2 cup whole or jellied cranberry sauce**

1 Arrange the turkey and watercress on top of bread.

2 Spread one side of the remaining bread slices with cranberry sauce. Place the bread on top of turkey and watercress, cranberry sides down. Cut each sandwich in half diagonally. Serve immediately. Makes 4 sandwiches.

Nutrition Facts per serving: 316 cal., 5 g total fat (1 g sat. fat), 34 mg chol., 331 mg sodium, 37 g carbo., 3 g fiber, 30 g pro.
Daily Values: 4% vit. C, 8% calcium, 16% iron
Exchanges: 2½ Starch, 3 Very Lean Meat

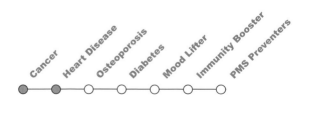

Cancer · Heart Disease · Osteoporosis · Diabetes · Mood Lifter · Immunity Booster · PMS Preventers

Grilled Turkey With Pepper Sauce   **Prep:** 20 minutes   **Grill:** 25 minutes

Loaded with vitamin C, red and yellow sweet peppers add natural sweetness to the savory sauce on top of these grilled turkey steaks. The peppers also increase immunity, lessen menopause symptoms, mitigate arthritis, and help protect against cancer and heart disease.

2	tablespoons olive oil or cooking oil
2	medium red or yellow sweet peppers, chopped
$1/2$	cup finely chopped onion
$3/4$	cup chicken broth
$1/4$	teaspoon salt
$1/4$	teaspoon black pepper
2	cloves garlic, minced
2	turkey breast tenderloins (about 1 pound total)
3	cups hot cooked mafalda or fettuccine
2	tablespoons finely shredded fresh basil

1 For sauce, in a large skillet heat 1 tablespoon of the oil over medium heat. Add sweet peppers and onion. Cook about 10 minutes or until vegetables are very tender, stirring occasionally. Transfer vegetables to a food processor bowl or blender container; add broth, salt, and black pepper. Cover and process or blend until mixture is smooth. Return to skillet; set aside.

2 In a small bowl combine the remaining 1 tablespoon oil and garlic. Brush over turkey.

3 In a grill with a cover arrange medium-hot coals around a drip pan. Test for medium heat above the pan. Place turkey on the grill rack over the drip pan. Cover and grill for 25 to 30 minutes or until turkey is tender and no longer pink.

4 Cut the turkey into slices. Reheat the sauce. Serve the turkey and sauce over pasta. Sprinkle with basil. If desired, garnish with additional basil. Makes 4 servings.

Nutrition Facts per serving: 380 cal., 9 g total fat (2 g sat. fat), 68 mg chol., 348 mg sodium, 38 g carbo., 3 g fiber, 34 g pro.
Daily Values: 62% vit. A, 153% vit. C, 4% calcium, 17% iron
Exchanges: 1 Vegetable, 2 Starch, 4 Very Lean Meat, $1/2$ Fat

Cancer   Heart Disease   Osteoporosis   Diabetes   Mood Lifter   Immunity Booster   PMS Preventers

Turkey With Tomatillo Guacamole

Prep: 15 minutes   **Grill:** 1¼ hours

Turkey contains the amino acid tryptophan, which helps trigger production of serotonin, a brain chemical that enhances mood and promotes sleep.

1	**2- to 3-pound fresh or frozen turkey breast portion**
2	**teaspoons ground coriander**
½	**teaspoon onion powder**
¼	**teaspoon chili powder**
	Dash ground red pepper
1	**tablespoon margarine or butter**
1	**tablespoon lemon juice**
1	**recipe Tomatillo Guacamole**

1 Thaw turkey, if frozen. Remove skin and excess fat from turkey. In a small saucepan cook coriander, onion powder, chili powder, and red pepper in hot margarine for 1 minute. Remove from heat; stir in lemon juice. Brush over turkey. Insert a meat thermometer into the thickest part of turkey, not touching bone (if present).

2 In a grill with a cover arrange medium-hot coals around a drip pan. Test for medium heat above the pan. Place turkey on the grill rack over the drip pan. Cover and grill for 1¼ to 1¾ hours or until thermometer registers 170°. Serve the turkey with Tomatillo Guacamole. Makes 8 servings.

Tomatillo Guacamole: In a small bowl stir together ½ of a small avocado, seeded, peeled, and chopped (about ½ cup); 2 canned tomatillos, rinsed, drained, and finely chopped (about ¼ cup); 1 plum tomato, chopped; 1 tablespoon canned diced green chile peppers; 2 teaspoons lemon juice; and ⅛ teaspoon garlic salt.

Nutrition Facts per serving: 156 cal., 6 g total fat (1 g sat. fat), 50 mg chol., 157 mg sodium, 3 g carbo., 0 g fiber, 22 g pro.
Daily Values: 34% vit. A, 5% vit. C, 27% calcium, 1% iron
Exchanges: ½ Vegetable, 3 Very Lean Meat, ½ Fat

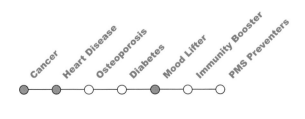

Turkey With Cranberry Sauce

Prep: 10 minutes   **Roast:** 2½ hours

Flavonoids give ruby cranberries their color and may protect against cancer and heart disease. Drinking a tall glass of cranberry juice daily helps stave off urinary tract infections too.

- 1   **2½- to 3-pound fresh or frozen turkey breast half with bone**
- 1½   **cups cranberries**
- ½   **cup coarsely shredded carrot**
- ½   **teaspoon finely shredded orange peel**
- ½   **cup orange juice**
- 2   **tablespoons sugar**
- 2   **tablespoons raisins**
- **Dash ground cloves**
- 1   **tablespoon cold water**
- 2   **teaspoons cornstarch**

1 Thaw turkey, if frozen. Remove skin and excess fat from turkey. Place turkey, bone side down, on a rack in a shallow roasting pan. Insert a meat thermometer into the thickest part of turkey, not touching bone. Cover turkey loosely with foil.

2 Roast in a 325° oven for 2½ to 3 hours or until thermometer registers 170°. Remove foil the last 30 minutes of roasting.

3 Meanwhile, for sauce, in a small saucepan combine cranberries, carrot, orange peel, orange juice, sugar, raisins, and cloves. Bring to boiling; reduce heat. Simmer, uncovered, for 3 to 4 minutes or until cranberry skins pop.

4 In a small bowl combine cold water and cornstarch; stir into cranberry mixture. Cook and stir until thickened and bubbly. Cook and stir for 2 minutes more. Serve the turkey with sauce. Makes 8 servings.

Nutrition Facts per serving: 154 cal., 2 g total fat (1 g sat. fat), 50 mg chol., 49 mg sodium, 11 g carbo., 1 g fiber, 22 g pro.
Daily Values: 19% vit. A, 19% vit. C, 1% calcium, 7% iron
Exchanges: 1 Fruit, 3 Very Lean Meat

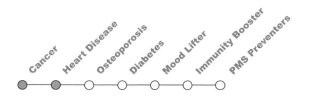

Southwestern Stuffed Squash

Prep: 15 minutes   **Bake:** 55 minutes

Butternut squash contains phenolic compounds, antioxidants that protect body cells by fighting off damaging free radicals and hindering harmful changes in LDL ("bad") cholesterol. Beta-carotene contributes to the squash's vivid orange color.

3	1½- to 2-pound butternut squash
8	ounces uncooked ground turkey or chicken
2	green onions, sliced
1	to 2 teaspoons chili powder
½	teaspoon dried oregano, crushed
1	15-ounce can black beans or pinto beans, rinsed and drained
1	8-ounce can tomato sauce
¼	cup sliced, pitted ripe olives (optional)
1	fresh jalapeño pepper, seeded and chopped*
	Light dairy sour cream (optional)

1 Cut off the blossom ends of squash. Cut off a shallow lengthwise slice from one side of each squash. Finely chop enough of the slices to equal ½ cup; set aside. Remove and discard seeds from cavities of squash. Hollow out squash, leaving ½-inch shells. Invert squash in a shallow baking pan. Bake, uncovered, in a 350° oven for 40 minutes or until squash are tender.

2 Meanwhile, in a large skillet cook turkey and chopped squash until turkey is brown. Stir in green onions, chili powder, and oregano. Cook and stir for 2 minutes. Stir in beans, tomato sauce, olives (if desired), and jalapeño pepper. Bring to boiling. Spoon the bean mixture into hollows of baked squash.

3 Bake, uncovered, in a 350° oven for 15 minutes or until heated through. If desired, serve with sour cream. Makes 6 servings.

Nutrition Facts per serving: 246 cal., 4 g total fat (1 g sat. fat), 30 mg chol., 447 mg sodium, 46 g carbo., 4 g fiber, 15 g pro.
Daily Values: 435% vit. A, 97% vit. C, 18% calcium, 21% iron
Exchanges: 2 Vegetable, 2 Starch, 1 Very Lean Meat

---

*Note: Hot peppers contain volatile oils in the seeds and inner membranes that can burn eyes, lips, and sensitive skin. Wear plastic gloves when handling hot peppers and wash your hands thoroughly with soap and water afterwards.

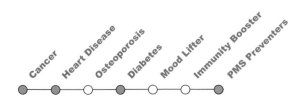

Cancer   Heart Disease   Osteoporosis   Diabetes   Mood Lifter   Immunity Booster   PMS Preventers

Mexican-Style Turkey Soup   **Prep:** 20 minutes   **Cook:** 20 minutes

This spicy soup provides health-protective phytochemicals in every bite. You'll get lutein and zeaxanthin from the corn and red sweet pepper, lycopene from the tomato, and beta-carotene from the winter squash. Tip: For maximum phytochemicals and health benefits, choose the most vivid fruits and vegetables.

1 cup chopped onion	1½ cups peeled, cubed winter squash
1 large red sweet pepper, chopped	1 large tomato, chopped
1 tablespoon cooking oil	¼ teaspoon salt
1 teaspoon ground cumin	¼ teaspoon black pepper
1 teaspoon chili powder	2 cups chopped cooked turkey or chicken
½ teaspoon paprika	1 cup frozen whole kernel corn
5 cups reduced-sodium chicken broth	2 tablespoons snipped fresh cilantro

1 In a Dutch oven cook onion and sweet pepper in hot oil over medium heat about 5 minutes or until tender, stirring occasionally. Stir in cumin, chili powder, and paprika; cook and stir for 30 seconds.

2 Add broth, squash, tomato, salt, and black pepper. Bring to boiling; reduce heat. Simmer, covered, about 20 minutes or until squash is tender, stirring occasionally. Stir in turkey, corn, and cilantro; heat through. Makes 5 or 6 servings.

Nutrition Facts per serving: 205 cal., 6 g total fat (1 g sat. fat), 43 mg chol., 790 mg sodium, 17 g carbo., 3 g fiber, 22 g pro.
Daily Values: 73% vit. A, 102% vit. C, 4% calcium, 10% iron
Exchanges: ½ Vegetable, 1 Starch, 2 Very Lean Meat, ½ Fat

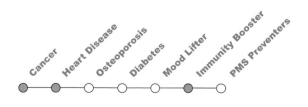

Cancer   Heart Disease   Osteoporosis   Diabetes   Mood Lifter   Immunity Booster   PMS Preventers

MeatlessMainDishes

Enoki Mushroom and Vegetable Cups, page 124

Enoki Mushroom And Vegetable Cups   **Start to Finish:** 25 minutes

Cabbage leaves filled with green onions, slaw mix, sweet pepper, and enoki mushrooms make a delicious, vegetable-packed wrap. Overcooking cabbage removes much of its cancer-fighting bonuses. Therefore, it's best to lightly cook cabbage, as in this recipe, to keep its health components intact. (Pictured on page 123.)

1   **teaspoon toasted sesame oil**

2   **teaspoons olive oil**

1   **cup fresh pea pods, trimmed and halved crosswise (about 2¹/₂ ounces)**

1   **medium red sweet pepper, cut into thin strips**

6   **green onions, cut into 1-inch pieces**

2   **3.2-ounce packages fresh enoki mushrooms**

3   **cups packaged shredded cabbage with carrot (coleslaw mix)**

¹/₄   **cup hoisin sauce**

4   **napa cabbage cups or 8-inch fat-free flour tortillas, warmed**

1 Pour sesame oil and olive oil into skillet. Heat skillet over medium heat. Add pea pods, sweet pepper, and green onions to skillet; cook and stir for 2 to 3 minutes or until vegetables are crisp-tender. Stir in mushrooms, cabbage, and hoisin sauce. Heat through.

2 Divide the mushroom mixture among cabbage cups or tortillas. Insert wooden skewers through cabbage cups to hold their shape, or roll up tortillas. Serve immediately. Makes 4 servings.

Nutrition Facts per serving: 240 cal., 4 g total fat (1 g sat. fat), 0 mg chol., 677 mg sodium, 45 g carbo., 6 g fiber, 5 g pro.
Daily Values: 52% vit. A, 153% vit. C, 10% calcium, 11% iron
Exchanges: 2¹/₂ Vegetable, 2 Starch, ¹/₂ Fat

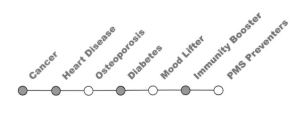

Stir-Fried Vegetables In Thai Peanut Sauce

Start to Finish: 25 minutes

Nutrient-dense peanuts and peanut butter are high in monounsaturated fat (a good thing) and contain vitamin E, folate, plant protein, and fiber. Peanuts also contain beta-sitosterol, which might help protect against colon, prostate, and breast cancers, and resveratrol, which may reduce the risk of heart disease and some cancers.

1/2	cup reduced-sodium chicken broth	2	medium carrots, cut into thin bite-size strips
1	fresh jalapeño pepper, seeded and finely chopped*	1	small onion, cut into thin wedges
1	clove garlic, minced	2	cups shredded napa cabbage
1/4	cup peanut butter	1	small cucumber, seeded and cut into thin bite-size strips
2	tablespoons rice vinegar	1	tablespoon snipped fresh Thai basil or mint
2	tablespoons reduced-sodium soy sauce	3	cups hot cooked jasmine or long grain rice
1	teaspoon toasted sesame oil	1/4	cup coarsely chopped unsalted dry roasted peanuts
1	tablespoon cooking oil		

1 For sauce, in a small saucepan stir together broth, jalapeño pepper, and garlic. Bring to boiling; reduce heat. Simmer, covered, about 2 minutes or until jalapeño pepper is tender. Add peanut butter; stir until combined. Remove from heat. Stir in rice vinegar, soy sauce, and sesame oil; set aside.

2 Pour cooking oil into a wok or large skillet. Heat wok over medium-high heat. Stir-fry carrots and onion in hot oil about 4 minutes or until vegetables are crisp-tender.

3 Add the sauce, cabbage, cucumber, and Thai basil. Reduce heat to medium-low. Cook and stir for 1 to 2 minutes or until heated through. Serve immediately over rice. Sprinkle each serving with peanuts. Makes 4 servings.

Nutrition Facts per serving: 350 cal., 18 g total fat (3 g sat. fat), 0 mg chol., 459 mg sodium, 39 g carbo., 4 g fiber, 11 g pro.
Daily Values: 165% vit. A, 29% vit. C, 7% calcium, 9% iron
Exchanges: 1½ Vegetable, 2 Starch, ½ High Fat Meat, 2½ Fat

---

*Note: Hot peppers contain volatile oils in the seeds and inner membranes that can burn eyes, lips, and sensitive skin. Wear plastic gloves when handling hot peppers and wash your hands thoroughly with soap and water afterwards.

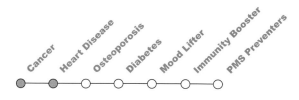

Cancer · Heart Disease · Osteoporosis · Diabetes · Mood Lifter · Immunity Booster · PMS Preventers

Herbed Pasta Primavera

Prep: 25 minutes   **Cook:** 13 minutes

Aromatic basil and dill complement this quartet of seasonal vegetables: summer squash, leeks, asparagus, and baby carrots. Abundant in beta-carotene, this dish promotes healthy skin.

6 **ounces dried mostaccioli**	1 **clove garlic, minced**
1 **cup water**	8 **ounces baby pattypan squash**
1 **tablespoon cornstarch**	2 **tablespoons water**
2 **teaspoons instant chicken bouillon granules**	1 **tablespoon snipped fresh basil or 1 teaspoon**
8 **ounces tiny whole carrots with tops (about 12)**	**dried basil, crushed**
Nonstick cooking spray	2 **teaspoons snipped fresh dill or ¹/₂ teaspoon**
1¹/₂ **cups green beans bias-sliced into 2-inch pieces**	**dried dillweed**
2 **medium leeks, halved lengthwise and sliced**	¹/₄ **cup chopped almonds, toasted**
¹/₄ inch thick	**Cracked black pepper**

1 Cook mostaccioli according to package directions; drain. Return mostaccioli to saucepan; cover and keep warm.

2 Meanwhile, for sauce, in a small bowl combine the 1 cup water, the cornstarch, and bouillon granules; set aside. If desired, cut off the tops of carrots. Halve carrots lengthwise.

3 Lightly coat a wok or large skillet with cooking spray. Heat wok over medium-high heat. Stir-fry carrots in hot wok for 5 minutes. Add green beans, leeks, and garlic. Stir-fry for 2 minutes more. Stir in squash and the 2 tablespoons water. Cook, covered, for 3 to 4 minutes or until vegetables are crisp-tender. Push vegetables from center of wok.

4 Stir sauce; add to center of wok. Cook and stir until thickened and bubbly. Add basil and dill. Stir all ingredients together to coat with sauce. Cook and stir for 1 to 2 minutes more or until heated through.

5 To serve, spoon the vegetable mixture over mostaccioli. Sprinkle with almonds and black pepper. Serve immediately. Makes 4 servings.

Nutrition Facts per serving: 272 cal., 5 g total fat (10 g sat. fat), 0 mg chol., 584 mg sodium, 48 g carbo., 6 g fiber, 10 g pro.
Daily Values: 265% vit. A, 30% vit. C, 8% calcium, 19% iron
Exchanges: 2 Vegetable, 2¹/₂ Starch, ¹/₂ Fat

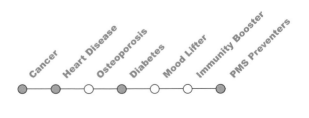

Wheat Fettuccine With Arugula

Start to Finish: 25 minutes

Arugula is a member of the cancer-preventive cruciferous vegetable family. It can be eaten raw in salads or lightly cooked. Cooking will slightly mellow arugula's spicy bite.

- 8 ounces dried whole wheat fettuccine
- 2 cloves garlic, minced
- 2 tablespoons olive oil
- $\frac{1}{4}$ cup chicken broth
- 3 tablespoons balsamic vinegar
- $\frac{1}{4}$ teaspoon salt
- $\frac{1}{8}$ teaspoon crushed red pepper
- 8 cups torn arugula
- 2 medium tomatoes, coarsely chopped
- $\frac{1}{3}$ cup finely shredded Parmesan cheese
- $\frac{1}{4}$ cup pine nuts, toasted

1 Cook fettuccine according to package directions; drain. Return fettuccine to saucepan; cover and keep warm.

2 Meanwhile, in a 12-inch skillet cook garlic in hot oil for 1 minute. Stir in broth, vinegar, salt, and crushed red pepper. Bring to boiling; remove skillet from heat. Stir in cooked fettuccine, arugula, and tomatoes.

3 To serve, divide the pasta mixture among 4 dinner plates. Sprinkle with Parmesan cheese and pine nuts. Serve immediately. Makes 4 servings.

Nutrition Facts per serving: 388 cal., 15 g total fat (4 g sat. fat), 8 mg chol., 316 mg sodium, 53 g carbo., 6 g fiber, 16 g pro.
Daily Values: 29% vit. A, 31% vit. C, 18% calcium, 22% iron
Exchanges: 2$\frac{1}{2}$ Vegetable, 2$\frac{1}{2}$ Starch, $\frac{1}{2}$ Lean Meat, 2 Fat

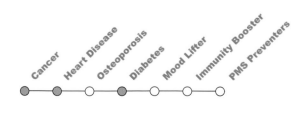

Cancer   Heart Disease   Osteoporosis   Diabetes   Mood Lifter   Immunity Booster   PMS Preventers

Udon Noodles With Bok Choy And Tofu

Start to Finish: 30 minutes

Bok choy—also called Chinese white cabbage—is a cruciferous vegetable, meaning it's loaded with cancer-preventive (especially breast cancer) plant compounds called indoles. Bok choy is also a source of easily absorbable calcium.

6 **ounces udon noodles**	1 **tablespoon grated fresh ginger**
¼ **cup reduced-sodium soy sauce**	2 **cloves garlic, minced**
2 **tablespoons honey**	1 **medium red sweet pepper, cut into thin strips**
1 **tablespoon oyster sauce**	6 **green onions, cut into 1-inch pieces**
1 **tablespoon balsamic vinegar**	6 **cups sliced bok choy**
2 **teaspoons cornstarch**	1 **12-ounce package extra-firm tofu (fresh bean curd), drained and**
1 **teaspoon toasted sesame oil**	**cut into ½-inch cubes**
1 **tablespoon cooking oil**	1 **8-ounce can sliced water chestnuts, drained**

1 Cook udon noodles according to package directions; drain. Return noodles to saucepan; cover and keep warm.

2 Meanwhile, for sauce, in a small bowl stir together soy sauce, honey, oyster sauce, vinegar, cornstarch, and sesame oil; set aside.

3 Pour cooking oil into a wok or large skillet. (Add more oil as necessary during cooking.) Heat wok over medium-high heat. Stir-fry ginger and garlic in hot oil for 15 seconds. Add sweet pepper and green onions. Stir-fry about 2 minutes or until sweet pepper is crisp-tender. Remove vegetables. Add bok choy, half at a time; stir-fry about 3 minutes or until crisp-tender. Remove bok choy. Add tofu; stir-fry for 4 minutes. Push tofu from center of wok.

4 Stir sauce; add to center of wok. Cook and stir until slightly thickened. Return all vegetables to wok. Add cooked noodles and water chestnuts. Stir all ingredients together to coat with sauce; heat through. Serve immediately. Makes 4 servings.

Nutrition Facts per serving: 385 cal., 10 g total fat (1 g sat. fat), 0 mg chol., 942 mg sodium, 66 g carbo., 3 g fiber, 14 g pro.
Daily Values: 87% vit. A, 154% vit. C, 35% calcium, 16% iron
Exchanges: 2 Vegetable, 3½ Starch, ½ Medium Fat Meat, 1 Fat

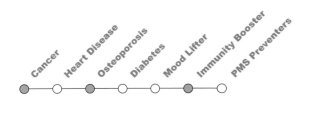

Pumpkin And Sage Risotto

Start to Finish: 40 minutes

The antioxidants beta-carotene and alpha-carotene mix with other carotenoids to give pumpkin its brilliant orange hue. Carotenoids appear to fight various types of cancer, such as stomach, esophageal, bladder, and breast. Carotenoids also boost immunity.

6	**cups reduced-sodium chicken broth**
½	**cup canned pumpkin**
1	**small onion, finely chopped**
1	**tablespoon olive oil**
3	**cups cubed, peeled pumpkin or butternut squash**
2	**cups arborio rice**
⅓	**cup dry white wine or reduced-sodium chicken broth**
½	**cup grated Parmesan cheese**
2	**teaspoons snipped fresh sage**
	Black pepper
	Hot cooked broccoli (optional)

1 In a large saucepan stir together broth and canned pumpkin. Bring to boiling; reduce heat. Simmer until needed.

2 Meanwhile, in a 4-quart Dutch oven cook onion in hot oil over medium heat about 5 minutes or until tender. Add fresh pumpkin; cook and stir for 2 minutes. Add uncooked rice. Cook and stir for 2 minutes more.

3 Slowly add wine to the rice mixture and cook until wine is evaporated. Slowly add 2 cups of the broth mixture, stirring constantly. Continue to cook and stir until liquid is absorbed. Add the remaining broth mixture, ¾ cup at a time, stirring constantly until the broth is absorbed. (This should take about 30 minutes.)

4 Stir the Parmesan cheese and sage into rice mixture. Season to taste with black pepper. If desired, serve the rice mixture over broccoli. Makes 6 to 8 servings.

Nutrition Facts per serving: 333 cal., 5 g total fat (2 g sat. fat), 7 mg chol., 781 mg sodium, 57 g carbo., 2 g fiber, 12 g pro.
Daily Values: 109% vit. A, 10% vit. C, 16% calcium, 20% iron
Exchanges: 1½ Vegetable, 3½ Starch, ½ Fat

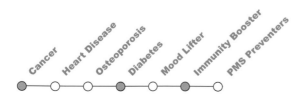

Spinach-Feta Bake

Prep: 20 minutes **Bake:** 30 minutes

Spinach is packed with the carotenoids lutein and zeaxanthin, compounds also found in the eye. Research suggests that frequent eating of spinach protects against age-related macular degeneration, the leading cause of blindness in people over 65.

Nonstick cooking spray	1 cup crumbled feta cheese (4 ounces)
³/₄ cup chopped onion	¹/₂ cup refrigerated or frozen egg product, thawed
3 cloves garlic, minced	1 tablespoon snipped fresh oregano or 1 teaspoon
1 teaspoon olive oil or cooking oil	dried oregano, crushed
2 10-ounce packages frozen chopped spinach,	¹/₄ teaspoon coarsely ground black pepper
thawed and well-drained	¹/₄ cup finely shredded Parmesan cheese
1 cup low-fat cottage cheese, drained	2 tablespoons fine dry bread crumbs

1 Lightly coat a 9-inch pie plate with cooking spray; set aside. In a medium saucepan cook onion and garlic in hot oil until onion is tender.

2 Stir spinach, drained cottage cheese, feta cheese, egg product, oregano, and black pepper into onion mixture. Spoon the spinach mixture into the prepared pie plate.

3 In a small bowl combine Parmesan cheese and bread crumbs; sprinkle over spinach mixture. Bake, uncovered, in a 350° oven for 30 to 35 minutes or until a knife inserted near center comes out clean. To serve, cut into wedges. Makes 6 servings.

Nutrition Facts per serving: 157 cal., 7 g total fat (4 g sat. fat), 24 mg chol., 621 mg sodium, 8 g carbo., 3 g fiber, 14 g pro.
Daily Values: 278% vit. A, 14% vit. C, 25% calcium, 6% iron
Exchanges: 1¹/₂ Vegetable, 1¹/₂ Medium Fat Meat

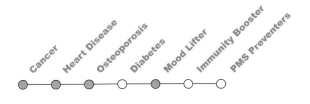

Vegetable Polenta Lasagna, page 134

Vegetable Polenta Lasagna

Prep: 25 minutes **Bake:** 40 minutes **Chill:** 1 hour

Polenta, a cornmeal mush commonly eaten in Northern Italy, makes an unusual alternative to noodles in this veggie-loaded lasagna. For the most fiber, vitamins, and minerals, purchase cornmeal labeled "water-ground" or "stone-ground." (Pictured on page 132.)

4 **cups cold water**	¼ **teaspoon freshly ground black pepper**
1½ **cups cornmeal**	3 **medium green sweet peppers, roasted and chopped***
1¼ **teaspoons salt**	3 **medium red sweet peppers, roasted and chopped***
1 **small onion, thinly sliced**	1¼ **cups marinara sauce**
1 **tablespoon olive oil**	1 **cup shredded mozzarella cheese (4 ounces)**
4 **cups fresh mushrooms, halved**	

1 For polenta, in a medium saucepan bring 2½ cups of the water to boiling. In a medium bowl combine the remaining 1½ cups water, the cornmeal, and 1 teaspoon of the salt. Slowly add cornmeal mixture to boiling water, stirring constantly. Cook and stir until mixture returns to boiling; reduce heat to low. Cook about 10 minutes or until mixture is very thick, stirring occasionally. Pour the hot mixture into a 3-quart rectangular baking dish. Cool slightly. Cover and refrigerate about 1 hour or until firm. (Or cover and refrigerate up to 24 hours.)

2 In a large nonstick skillet cook onion in hot oil over medium heat for 3 to 4 minutes or until tender. Add mushrooms, the remaining ¼ teaspoon salt, and the black pepper. Cook and stir about 5 minutes or until mushrooms are tender. Remove from heat; stir in the green and red roasted sweet peppers.

3 Spread the marinara sauce over chilled polenta. Top with the vegetable mixture and sprinkle with mozzarella cheese. Bake, covered, in a 350° oven for 30 minutes. Bake, uncovered, for 10 to 15 minutes more or until edges are bubbly. Makes 8 servings.

Nutrition Facts per serving: 203 cal., 6 g total fat (2 g sat. fat), 8 mg chol., 597 mg sodium, 31 g carbo., 5 g fiber, 8 g pro.
Daily Values: 57% vit. A, 172% vit. C, 11% calcium, 11% iron
Exchanges: 2 Vegetable, 1½ Starch, ½ Medium Fat Meat, ½ Fat

---

*Note: To roast peppers, quarter the peppers lengthwise; remove stems, seeds, and membranes. Place peppers, cut sides down, on a foil-lined baking sheet. Roast in a 450° oven for 15 to 20 minutes or until skins are blistered and bubbly. Fold up foil on baking sheet around peppers to form a packet; seal. Let stand for 20 minutes to loosen skins. Peel and chop peppers. (Or substitute three 7-ounce jars or two 12-ounce jars roasted red sweet peppers, drained and chopped, for the green and red sweet peppers.)

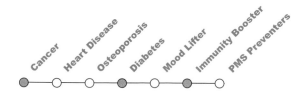

Mediterranean Fregola   **Start to Finish:** 25 minutes

A traditional dish in Italy, fregola isn't a grain but a tiny pasta pellet made from semolina and water. Fregola and garbanzo beans pair up in this meatless dish to provide a complete source of protein. (Pictured on page 133.)

6	cups water	1/4	teaspoon black pepper
1	tablespoon instant chicken bouillon granules	1	tablespoon small fresh oregano leaves or 1 teaspoon
1 1/2	cups fregola (Italian couscous) or dried orzo pasta		dried oregano, crushed
	(rosamarina)	1	clove garlic, minced
1	tablespoon olive oil	2	cups chopped plum tomatoes
1	medium red onion, halved lengthwise and thinly sliced	1	15-ounce can garbanzo beans, rinsed and drained
2	medium zucchini and/or yellow summer squash, halved	1/2	cup crumbled feta cheese (2 ounces)
	lengthwise and sliced 1/4 inch thick		Fresh oregano leaves (optional)
1/4	teaspoon salt		

1 In a large saucepan bring water and bouillon granules to boiling. Add fregola. Cook according to package directions; drain. Transfer to a large bowl. Drizzle with 1 teaspoon of the oil; toss to coat. Cover and keep warm.

2 Meanwhile, in a large nonstick skillet heat the remaining 2 teaspoons oil over medium heat. Add onion; cook for 2 minutes. Add zucchini, salt, and black pepper. Cook for 3 to 4 minutes or just until zucchini is tender, stirring frequently. Stir in oregano and garlic; cook for 1 minute more. Stir in tomatoes and garbanzo beans; heat through.

3 Spoon the vegetable mixture over fregola; toss gently to coat. Divide among 4 bowls or dinner plates. Sprinkle with feta cheese. If desired, garnish with additional fresh oregano leaves. Serve immediately. Makes 4 servings.

Nutrition Facts per serving: 430 cal., 10 g total fat (3 g sat. fat), 13 mg chol., 1,268 mg sodium, 72 g carbo., 5 g fiber, 17 g pro.
Daily Values: 16% vit. A, 37% vit. C, 13% calcium, 12% iron
Exchanges: 1 Vegetable, 4 1/2 Starch, 1/2 Medium Fat Meat, 1/2 Fat

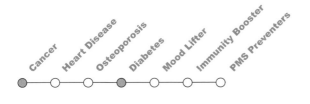

Aloo Ghobi   **Start to Finish:** 30 minutes

Veggies brimming with cancer-fighting lycopene, beta-carotene, allium compounds, and indoles abound in this fragrant, Indian-spiced stew. Serve it over brown rice for extra fiber and energy-boosting whole-grain goodness.

1 large red onion, halved lengthwise and thinly sliced	2 medium potatoes, peeled and cut into 1-inch cubes (1½ cups)
1 tablespoon olive oil	2 medium sweet potatoes, peeled and cut into 1-inch cubes (1½ cups)
2 teaspoons curry powder	1½ cups vegetable broth or water
1 teaspoon ground cumin	¼ teaspoon salt
¼ teaspoon garam masala	¼ teaspoon freshly ground black pepper
⅛ teaspoon ground red pepper	1 cup frozen peas
3 cups medium cauliflower florets	4½ cups hot cooked brown rice or couscous
1 14½-ounce can diced tomatoes, undrained	

1 In a large saucepan cook onion in hot oil over medium heat about 5 minutes or until tender. Add curry powder, cumin, garam masala, and red pepper. Cook and stir for 1 minute.

2 Stir in cauliflower, tomatoes, potatoes, sweet potatoes, broth, salt, and black pepper. Bring to boiling; reduce heat. Simmer, covered, for 10 to 12 minutes or until potatoes are tender. Stir in peas; heat through. Serve stew over hot brown rice. Makes 6 servings.

Nutrition Facts per serving: 334 cal., 4 g total fat (1 g sat. fat), 0 mg chol., 510 mg sodium, 66 g carbo., 9 g fiber, 9 g pro.
Daily Values: 224% vit. A, 84% vit. C, 9% calcium, 13% iron
Exchanges: 1 Vegetable, 4 Starch

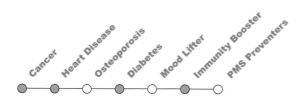

Tabbouleh-Style Couscous With Tofu   **Start to Finish:** 25 minutes

Tofu contains alpha-linolenic acid, a type of omega-3 fatty acid found in soy foods and canola oil. One study showed that heart attack patients who consumed a diet high in alpha-linolenic acid for five years were less likely to suffer subsequent heart attacks.

1⅓ cups reduced-sodium chicken broth or vegetable broth	2 cloves garlic, minced
1 cup quick-cooking couscous	1½ cups chopped tomatoes
2 tablespoons olive oil	¼ cup snipped fresh basil
1 16-ounce package extra-firm tofu (fresh bean curd), drained and cut into ½-inch cubes	¼ cup lemon juice
⅔ cup sliced green onions	1 tablespoon snipped fresh mint
	¼ teaspoon black pepper
	½ cup crumbled feta cheese (2 ounces)

1 In a medium saucepan bring broth to boiling. Stir in couscous. Remove saucepan from heat. Cover and let stand for 5 minutes or until liquid is absorbed.

2 Meanwhile, in a large nonstick skillet heat 1 tablespoon of the oil over medium-high heat. Add tofu, green onions, and garlic. Cook for 8 to 10 minutes or until tofu is light brown, turning carefully. (If necessary, reduce heat to medium to prevent overbrowning.)

3 In a large bowl combine the couscous, tofu mixture, the remaining 1 tablespoon oil, the tomatoes, basil, lemon juice, mint, and black pepper; toss gently to coat. Sprinkle each serving with feta cheese. Makes 6 servings.

Nutrition Facts per serving: 264 cal., 10 g total fat (3 g sat. fat), 8 mg chol., 257 mg sodium, 30 g carbo., 3 g fiber, 14 g pro.
Daily Values: 9% vit. A, 28% vit. C, 18% calcium, 11% iron
Exchanges: 2 Starch, 1 Medium Fat Meat, ½ Fat

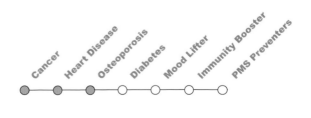

Fried Tofu And Watercress Salad

Start to Finish: 30 minutes

Tofu with a crispy, crunchy coating tops this ginger-spiked, medley-of-greens salad, creating a nutritional powerhouse. Rich in carotenoids, both spinach and watercress help save eyesight, lift moods, and fight cancer. Tofu fights cancer, decreases symptoms of menopause, builds bones, and battles heart disease.

1 **12-ounce package light, extra-firm tofu (fresh bean curd), drained**	$\frac{1}{3}$ **cup cooking oil**
3 **tablespoons tamari sauce or reduced-sodium soy sauce**	$\frac{1}{3}$ **cup cornmeal**
$\frac{1}{3}$ **cup rice vinegar**	1 **tablespoon sesame seeds, toasted**
2 **tablespoons grated fresh ginger**	2 **teaspoons cooking oil**
1 **tablespoon sugar**	6 **cups torn spinach**
1 **teaspoon Dijon-style mustard or $\frac{1}{4}$ teaspoon dry mustard**	1 **bunch watercress (about 1$\frac{1}{2}$ cups)**
$\frac{1}{4}$ **teaspoon salt**	1 **cup sliced fresh button mushrooms or enoki mushrooms**
	1 **cup red and/or yellow cherry tomatoes**
	1 **medium red onion, halved lengthwise and thinly sliced**

1 Cut tofu crosswise into eight $\frac{1}{2}$-inch slices. In a 2-quart rectangular baking dish arrange slices in a single layer. Pour tamari sauce over tofu; turn slices to coat. Let stand for 15 minutes.

2 Meanwhile, for vinaigrette, in a blender container or food processor bowl combine vinegar, ginger, sugar, mustard, and salt. Cover and blend or process until combined. With blender or processor running, add the $\frac{1}{3}$ cup oil in a thin steady stream. Blend or process for 15 seconds more.

3 Drain tofu, discarding tamari sauce. In a shallow dish combine cornmeal and sesame seeds. Carefully dip tofu slices in cornmeal mixture to lightly coat both sides. In a large nonstick skillet cook tofu in the 2 teaspoons hot oil for 5 to 6 minutes or until crisp and hot, carefully turning once. (You may need to cook tofu in two batches; avoid crowding the skillet.)

4 In an extra-large bowl combine spinach, watercress, mushrooms, tomatoes, and red onion. Pour the vinaigrette over spinach mixture; toss to coat. Divide among 4 dinner plates. Cut the tofu slices in half diagonally. Arrange the tofu over spinach mixture. If desired, sprinkle with additional sesame seeds. Makes 4 servings.

Nutrition Facts per serving: 330 cal., 23 g total fat (3 g sat. fat), 0 mg chol., 1,030 mg sodium, 21 g carbo., 6 g fiber, 11 g pro.
Daily Values: 70% vit. A, 50% vit. C, 9% calcium, 30% iron
Exchanges: 2 Vegetable, $\frac{1}{2}$ Starch, 1 Medium Fat Meat, 3$\frac{1}{2}$ Fat

Egg And Vegetable Salad Wraps

Start to Finish: 30 minutes

Need an energy boost? High-protein eggs wrapped with crisp, refreshing veggies are the perfect solution. Good for lunch or a light supper, the combination is also great for staving off menopausal problems and fighting infection.

4	hard-cooked eggs, chopped	2	tablespoons Dijon-style mustard
1	cup chopped cucumber	1	tablespoon fat-free milk
1	cup chopped zucchini or yellow summer squash	1	teaspoon snipped fresh tarragon or basil
½	cup chopped red onion	⅛	teaspoon paprika
½	cup shredded carrot	6	leaf lettuce leaves
¼	cup fat-free or light mayonnaise dressing or salad dressing	6	10-inch spinach, vegetable, or plain flour tortillas
		2	plum tomatoes, thinly sliced

1 In a large bowl combine eggs, cucumber, zucchini, red onion, and carrot. For dressing, in a small bowl stir together mayonnaise dressing, mustard, milk, tarragon, and paprika. Pour the dressing over egg mixture; toss gently to coat.

2 For each wrap, place a lettuce leaf on a tortilla. Place 3 or 4 tomato slices on top of the lettuce, slightly off center. Spoon about ⅔ cup of the egg mixture on top of the tomato slices. Fold in two opposite sides of the tortilla; roll up from the bottom. Cut the tortilla rolls in half diagonally. Makes 6 wraps.

Nutrition Facts per wrap: 307 cal., 8 g total fat (1 g sat. fat), 143 mg chol., 769 mg sodium, 46 g carbo., 2 g fiber, 13 g pro.
Daily Values: 71% vit. A, 18% vit. C, 10% calcium, 18% iron
Exchanges: 2 Vegetable, 2 Starch, 1 Medium Fat Meat, ½ Fat

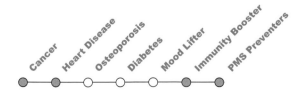

Swiss Chard And Potato Frittata   **Start to Finish:** 25 minutes

A member of the beet family, Swiss chard contains the carotenoids lutein, zeaxanthin, and beta-carotene. Chard contains calcium, but it's not absorbed well enough to count as a good source.

3	medium red potatoes, peeled
4	eggs
3	egg whites
¼	cup chopped fresh chives
2	tablespoons finely shredded Parmesan cheese
2	tablespoons fat-free milk
¼	teaspoon freshly ground black pepper
1	medium onion, thinly sliced
1	tablespoon olive oil
4	cups chopped Swiss chard

1 In a covered medium saucepan cook potatoes in a small amount of boiling, lightly salted water for 10 to 12 minutes or until tender; drain. Chop potatoes. In a medium bowl beat together the eggs, egg whites, chives, Parmesan cheese, milk, and black pepper. Stir in potatoes; set aside.

2 In a large nonstick skillet cook onion in hot oil over medium heat about 5 minutes or until tender. Add Swiss chard. Cook about 15 minutes or until liquid is evaporated, stirring frequently.

3 Pour egg mixture into skillet over Swiss chard mixture; do not stir. Cook over medium-low heat. As the egg mixture sets, run a spatula around edge of skillet, lifting egg mixture so the uncooked portion flows underneath. Continue cooking and lifting edges until the egg mixture is almost set (top will be wet). Cook, covered, about 3 minutes more or just until top is set. Cut into wedges. Serve immediately. Makes 6 servings.

Nutrition Facts per serving: 157 cal., 6 g total fat (2 g sat. fat), 143 mg chol., 155 mg sodium, 17 g carbo., 2 g fiber, 9 g pro.
Daily Values: 21% vit. A, 19% vit. C, 7% calcium, 7% iron
Exchanges: 1 Starch, 1 Medium Fat Meat

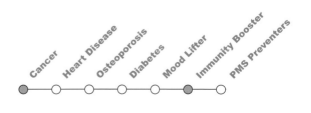

Two-Bean Burritos

Prep: 20 minutes **Cook:** 10 minutes

Hearty, high-protein beans are an abundant source of saponins. Preliminary research suggests that these compounds may stop cancer cells from multiplying, and they may help control blood sugar, cholesterol, and triglyceride levels.

6 10-inch spinach flour tortillas	2 tablespoons lime juice
1 15-ounce can black beans, rinsed and drained	1 fresh jalapeño pepper, seeded and finely chopped*
1 8¾-ounce can whole kernel corn, rinsed and drained	½ cup chopped onion
1 medium mango, chopped (1 cup)	2 teaspoons olive oil or cooking oil
⅓ cup chopped red sweet pepper	1 16-ounce can vegetarian refried beans
¼ cup snipped fresh cilantro	½ cup salsa

1 Wrap the tortillas in foil. Heat in a 350° oven about 10 minutes or until warm.

2 Meanwhile, in a medium bowl combine half of the black beans, the corn, mango, sweet pepper, cilantro, lime juice, and jalapeño pepper. Set aside until ready to serve.

3 In a large skillet cook onion in hot oil about 5 minutes or until tender. Stir in the remaining black beans, the refried beans, and salsa; heat through.

4 Divide the refried bean mixture among the warm tortillas; roll up. Top each serving with corn mixture. Makes 6 servings.

Nutrition Facts per serving: 308 cal., 7 g total fat (1 g sat. fat), 0 mg chol., 871 mg sodium, 69 g carbo., 9 g fiber, 12 g pro.
Daily Values: 37% vit. A, 53% vit. C, 11% calcium, 16% iron
Exchanges: ½ Fruit, 3 Starch, 1 Very Lean Meat, ½ Fat

---

*Note: Hot peppers contain volatile oils in the seeds and inner membranes that can burn eyes, lips, and sensitive skin. Wear plastic gloves when handling hot peppers and wash your hands thoroughly with soap and water afterwards.

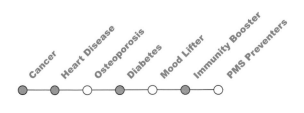

Risotto With Beans And Vegetables   **Start to Finish:** 30 minutes

Arborio rice cooks to a creamy consistency and offers energy-boosting complex carbohydrates. Using canned beans is a convenient way to boost your intake of soluble fiber, which helps lower blood cholesterol levels.

- **3 cups mushroom broth or vegetable broth**
- **2 cups sliced fresh mushrooms**
- **1 medium onion, chopped**
- **2 cloves garlic, minced**
- **2 tablespoons olive oil**
- **1 cup arborio rice**
- **1 cup finely chopped zucchini**
- **1 cup finely chopped carrots**
- **1 15-ounce can white kidney (cannellini) beans or**
  pinto beans, rinsed and drained
- **1/2 cup grated Parmesan cheese**
- **2 tablespoons snipped fresh Italian flat-leaf parsley**

1 In a medium saucepan bring broth to boiling. Reduce heat; simmer until needed. Meanwhile, in a large saucepan cook mushrooms, onion, and garlic in hot oil over medium heat about 5 minutes or until onion is tender. Add uncooked rice. Cook and stir about 5 minutes more or until rice is golden brown.

2 Slowly add 1 cup of the broth to the rice mixture, stirring constantly. Continue to cook and stir until liquid is absorbed. Add another 1/2 cup of the broth, the zucchini, and carrots to rice mixture, stirring constantly. Continue to cook and stir until liquid is absorbed. Add another 1 cup broth, 1/2 cup at a time, stirring constantly until the broth is absorbed. (This should take about 20 minutes.)

3 Stir the remaining 1/2 cup broth into rice mixture. Cook and stir until rice is slightly creamy and just tender. Stir in beans and Parmesan cheese; heat through. Sprinkle with parsley. Makes 4 servings.

Nutrition Facts per serving: 333 cal., 11 g total fat (3 g sat. fat), 10 mg chol., 585 mg sodium, 49 g carbo., 7 g fiber, 17 g pro.
Daily Values: 159% vit. A, 18% vit. C, 22% calcium, 24% iron
Exchanges: 3 Starch, 1 Very Lean Meat, 1 1/2 Fat

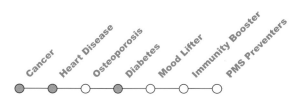

Mushroom and Asparagus Fettuccine, page 146

Herb and Bean-Stuffed Tomatoes, page 147

Mushroom And Asparagus Fettuccine

Start to Finish: 25 minutes

Like aspirin, mushrooms contain salicylates, which have an anticlotting effect on the blood. Shiitake mushrooms contain lentinan, which is thought to fight cancer. Asparagus contains the B-vitamin folacin, which helps fight heart disease and prevent birth defects. (Pictured on page 144.)

8 **ounces dried fettuccine or linguine**	¼ **teaspoon salt**
8 **ounces asparagus, trimmed and cut into 1½-inch pieces**	⅛ **teaspoon black pepper**
3 **cups sliced fresh shiitake or crimini mushrooms**	1 **cup chopped plum tomatoes**
1 **medium leek, thinly sliced, or ½ cup chopped onion**	1 **tablespoon finely shredded fresh basil**
3 **cloves garlic, minced**	1 **tablespoon finely shredded fresh oregano**
1 **tablespoon olive oil**	¼ **cup pine nuts, toasted**
⅓ **cup mushroom broth or vegetable broth**	**Finely shredded Parmesan cheese (optional)**
¼ **cup half-and-half or light cream**	

1 Cook fettuccine or linguine according to package directions, adding asparagus the last 1 to 2 minutes of cooking; drain. Return pasta mixture to saucepan; cover and keep warm.

2 Meanwhile, in a large skillet cook mushrooms, leek, and garlic in hot oil over medium-high heat for 4 to 5 minutes or until most of the liquid is evaporated. Stir in broth, half-and-half, salt, and black pepper. Bring to boiling. Boil gently, uncovered, for 4 to 5 minutes or until mixture is slightly thickened. Stir in tomatoes, basil, and oregano; heat through.

3 Spoon the mushroom mixture over pasta mixture; toss gently to coat. Divide among 4 bowls or dinner plates. Sprinkle with pine nuts and, if desired, Parmesan cheese. Serve immediately. Makes 4 servings.

Nutrition Facts per serving: 416 cal., 12 g total fat (3 g sat. fat), 6 mg chol., 193 mg sodium, 69 g carbo., 6 g fiber, 15 g pro.
Daily Values: 16% vit. A, 33% vit. C, 7% calcium, 25% iron
Exchanges: 2 Vegetable, 4 Starch, 1½ Fat

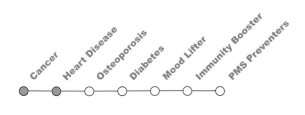

Herb And Bean-Stuffed Tomatoes

Prep: 25 minutes **Bake:** 20 minutes

Basil and thyme work with Parmesan cheese and garlic to confer the flavors of Italy on these bean-stuffed tomatoes. Legumes like cannellini beans are rich in dietary fiber and isoflavones, making them fighters of cancer, heart disease, and diabetes. (Pictured on page 145.)

4	large red and/or yellow tomatoes	1	tablespoon olive oil
1½	cups soft bread crumbs (2 slices)	2	cloves garlic, minced
½	of a 15-ounce can white kidney	⅛	teaspoon salt
	(cannellini) beans, rinsed and drained	⅛	teaspoon black pepper
¼	cup pine nuts, toasted	2	teaspoons snipped fresh thyme or ½ teaspoon
2	tablespoons grated Parmesan cheese		dried thyme, crushed
1	tablespoon finely shredded fresh basil or	2	teaspoons margarine or butter, melted
	½ teaspoon dried basil, crushed		

1 Cut off ½ inch from the top of each tomato. Finely chop enough of the tops to equal 1 cup; set aside. Remove and discard the seeds from tomatoes.

2 In a large bowl stir together the chopped tomato, ¾ cup of the bread crumbs, the beans, pine nuts, Parmesan cheese, basil, oil, garlic, salt, and black pepper. Spoon the bean mixture into the tomatoes. Place the stuffed tomatoes in a 2-quart square baking dish.

3 In a small bowl stir together the remaining ¾ cup bread crumbs and the thyme. Sprinkle bread crumb mixture over tomatoes. Drizzle with melted margarine.

4 Bake, uncovered, in a 350° oven about 20 minutes or until crumbs are golden brown and tomatoes are heated through. Makes 4 servings.

Nutrition Facts per serving: 220 cal., 12 g total fat (3 g sat. fat), 5 mg chol., 327 mg sodium, 25 g carbo., 5 g fiber, 9 g pro.
Daily Values: 22% vit. A, 51% vit. C, 8% calcium, 16% iron
Exchanges: 1½ Vegetable, 1 Starch, ½ Very Lean Meat, 2 Fat

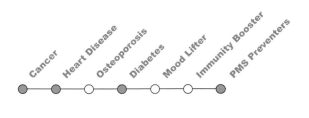

Indian-Style Sweet Potato Patties   **Start to Finish:** 25 minutes

Hot, spicy patties made from sweet potatoes and corn provide lots of beta-carotene, vitamin C, and vitamin E—great for preventing cancer, heart disease, and cataracts. They also advance immunity, decrease premenstrual syndrome, and diminish menopausal symptoms.

1 **beaten egg**	1/2 **cup fine dry bread crumbs or cornflake crumbs**
1 **fresh jalapeño pepper, seeded and finely chopped**	1/2 **cup firmly packed spinach leaves, finely chopped**
2 **cloves garlic, minced**	1/3 **cup sliced green onions**
1 **teaspoon ground cumin**	1/4 **cup snipped fresh cilantro**
1/2 **teaspoon ground ginger**	2 **teaspoons olive oil**
1/4 **teaspoon salt**	1/2 **cup mango chutney**
1 **large sweet potato, peeled and coarsely shredded**	1/2 **cup plain low-fat yogurt**
1 **cup frozen whole kernel corn, thawed**	

1 In a large bowl combine egg, jalapeño pepper, garlic, cumin, ginger, and salt.

2 Place shredded sweet potato on several layers of clean, white paper towels, firmly pressing to remove excess moisture. Add the sweet potato, corn, bread crumbs, spinach, green onions, and cilantro to egg mixture; mix well. Shape the potato mixture into eight 3-inch patties.

3 In a large nonstick skillet heat oil over medium heat. Cook patties, half at a time, in hot oil about 8 minutes or until golden brown, turning once. Serve the potato patties with chutney and yogurt. Makes 4 servings.

Nutrition Facts per serving: 293 cal., 5 g total fat (1 g sat. fat), 54 mg chol., 503 mg sodium, 59 g carbo., 4 g fiber, 7 g pro.
Daily Values: 220% vit. A, 52% vit. C, 13% calcium, 9% iron
Exchanges: 3½ Starch, ½ Fat

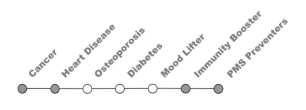

Zucchini-Carrot Burgers   **Start to Finish:** 25 minutes

These veggie burgers are a nutrient- and fiber-filled alternative to meat. Serving them in whole wheat pita bread ups your intake of whole grains. Health experts recommend consuming at least three daily servings of whole-grain foods to help prevent cancer and heart disease.

1/4 cup refrigerated or frozen egg product, thawed	1/2 cup plain low-fat yogurt
1 tablespoon olive oil	1 clove garlic, minced
1 teaspoon dried oregano, crushed	1/2 teaspoon finely shredded lemon peel
22 stone-ground wheat crackers, crushed (1 cup)	2 whole wheat pita bread rounds, halved
1 cup finely shredded zucchini	1 cup shredded leaf lettuce
1 cup finely shredded carrots	1 small tomato, thinly sliced
1/4 cup chopped green onions	1/2 of a small cucumber, thinly sliced

1 In a medium bowl combine egg product, 1 teaspoon of the oil, and the oregano. Add the crushed crackers, zucchini, carrots, and green onions to egg mixture; mix well. Shape the vegetable mixture into four 3½-inch patties.

2 In a large nonstick skillet heat the remaining 2 teaspoons oil over medium heat. Cook patties in hot oil for 5 to 7 minutes or until golden brown, turning once. Meanwhile, for sauce, in a small bowl combine the yogurt, garlic, and lemon peel.

3 To serve, fill the pita bread halves with vegetable burgers. Add the lettuce, tomato, cucumber, and sauce. Makes 4 servings.

Nutrition Facts per serving: 251 cal., 8 g total fat (2 g sat. fat), 2 mg chol., 365 mg sodium, 38 g carbo., 5 g fiber, 9 g pro.
Daily Values: 180% vit. A, 22% vit. C, 11% calcium, 16% iron
Exchanges: 1½ Vegetable, 2 Starch, 1 Fat

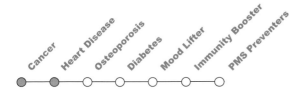

SideDishes

Italian-Style Vegetables, page 152

Italian-Style Vegetables

Prep: 10 minutes **Cook:** 5 minutes **Chill:** 4 hours

Artichoke hearts, lima beans, and sugar snap peas give this dill-seasoned combination an Italian accent. The beautiful vegetable combination fights cancer, and all three vegetables contain fiber and folate to reduce the risk of heart disease, tame diabetes, and prevent birth defects. (Pictured on page 151.)

1   **10-ounce package frozen lima beans**

1   **8-ounce package frozen sugar snap peas or one 9-ounce**

    package frozen Italian green beans

1   **6-ounce jar marinated artichoke hearts, undrained**

1   **tablespoon snipped fresh dill**

1/8 **teaspoon crushed red pepper**

    Romaine lettuce leaves

1   **green onion, thinly sliced**

    Fresh dill (optional)

    Lemon wedges (optional)

1 In a medium saucepan cook lima beans and snap peas in a small amount of boiling water for 5 to 8 minutes or until crisp-tender; drain. Rinse with cold water; drain again.

2 In a medium bowl combine the lima bean mixture, artichoke hearts, dill, and red pepper. Cover and refrigerate for 4 to 24 hours.

3 To serve, place the romaine leaves in a salad bowl. Spoon the lima bean mixture over romaine leaves. Sprinkle with sliced green onion. If desired, garnish with additional fresh dill and serve with lemon wedges. Makes 5 or 6 servings.

Nutrition Facts per serving: 114 cal., 4 g total fat (1 g sat. fat), 0 mg chol., 48 mg sodium, 17 g carbo., 6 g fiber, 5 g pro.
Daily Values: 21% vit. A, 33% vit. C, 6% calcium, 7% iron
Exchanges: 1/2 Vegetable, 1 Starch, 1/2 Fat

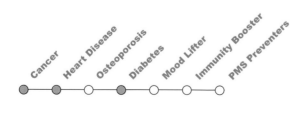

Roasted Ratatouille

Prep: 15 minutes   **Roast:** 28 minutes

Eggplant is a traditional ingredient in this dish from France. This deep purple fruit (yes, it's a fruit) is a good source of flavonoids, which may help protect cells from carcinogens, fend off harmful changes in LDL ("bad") cholesterol, and prevent blood clotting. Serve as a side dish with or without bread.

Nonstick cooking spray	**2 cloves garlic, minced**
1 small eggplant, cubed (3$\frac{1}{2}$ cups)	**$\frac{1}{8}$ teaspoon salt**
1 small zucchini or yellow summer squash, cubed (1 cup)	**$\frac{1}{8}$ teaspoon black pepper**
1 large onion, chopped	**2 large tomatoes, chopped**
1 medium yellow sweet pepper, cut into 1-inch strips	**1$\frac{1}{2}$ teaspoons lemon juice**
2 tablespoons snipped fresh Italian flat-leaf parsley or regular parsley	**Italian flat bread (focaccia), cut into wedges, or sliced French bread, toasted (optional)**
1 tablespoon olive oil	

1 Coat a 15×10×1-inch baking pan with cooking spray. Place eggplant, zucchini, onion, sweet pepper, and parsley in the prepared baking pan.

2 In a small bowl stir together oil, garlic, salt, and black pepper. Drizzle over vegetables; toss to coat.

3 Roast, uncovered, in a 450° oven about 20 minutes or until vegetables are tender and light brown, stirring once. Stir in the tomatoes and lemon juice. Roast, uncovered, for 8 to 10 minutes more or until tomatoes are soft and starting to juice out.

4 If desired, spoon the roasted vegetables onto the wedges of bread. Makes 4 servings.

Nutrition Facts per serving (without focaccia or bread): 120 cal., 5 g total fat (1 g sat. fat), 2 mg chol., 141 mg sodium, 18 g carbo., 4 g fiber, 4 g pro.
Daily Values: 109% vit. C, 6% calcium, 7% iron
Exchanges: 3 Vegetable, 1 Fat

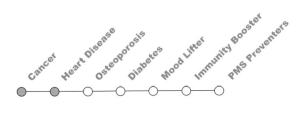

Arugula-Fennel Salad With Pear Vinaigrette

Start to Finish: 25 minutes

Fresh, sweet, crisp pears loaded with soluble fiber are tossed with calcium- and potassium-rich fennel for a salad packed with great taste and heart-protection synergy. Soluble fiber also helps regulate diabetes.

²/₃ **cup pear nectar**

3 **tablespoons seasoned rice vinegar**

1 **tablespoon olive oil**

½ **teaspoon coarsely ground black pepper**

1 **fennel bulb**

2 **cups arugula leaves**

2 **cups romaine lettuce leaves**

2 **small ripe pears, cored and thinly sliced**

½ **of a small red onion, thinly sliced and separated into rings**

¼ **cup broken walnuts, toasted**

1 **ounce Parmesan cheese**

1 For vinaigrette, in a small bowl whisk together pear nectar, vinegar, oil, and pepper. Set aside.

2 Cut off and discard upper stalks of fennel, reserving some feathery leaves for garnish (if desired). Remove wilted tough outer layer of stalks and cut off a thin slice from base of bulb. Cut the bulb in half lengthwise. Cut crosswise into thin slices, removing core (if desired).

3 In a medium bowl toss together sliced fennel, arugula, and romaine leaves. Pour about half of the vinaigrette over fennel mixture; toss to coat. Arrange the fennel mixture on 4 salad plates. Top with pears, red onion, and walnuts.

4 Use a vegetable peeler to thinly shave Parmesan cheese. Top the salads with shaved cheese and, if desired, garnish with fennel leaves. Drizzle with the remaining vinaigrette. Makes 4 servings.

Nutrition Facts per serving: 217 cal., 11 g total fat (2 g sat. fat), 6 mg chol., 282 mg sodium, 28 g carbo., 5 g fiber, 6 g pro.
Daily Values: 22% vit. A, 33% vit. C, 17% calcium, 9% iron
Exchanges: 1 Vegetable, 1½ Fruit, 2 Fat

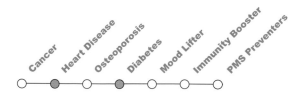

White Corn And Baby Pea Salad

Prep: 15 minutes   **Chill:** 1 hour

This vibrant salad couldn't be easier, because it uses frozen corn and peas. It is colorful, easy, and, of course, healthful.

1 **16-ounce package frozen white whole kernel corn (shoe peg), thawed**	½ **cup seasoned rice vinegar**
1 **16-ounce package frozen baby peas, thawed**	2 **tablespoons brown sugar**
1 **cup peeled and chopped jicama**	1 **tablespoon snipped fresh parsley**
⅔ **cup chopped celery**	½ **teaspoon salt**
½ **cup thinly sliced green onions**	¼ **teaspoon ground white pepper**
¼ **cup chopped red and/or orange sweet pepper**	1 **tablespoon snipped fresh mint**

1 In a large bowl combine corn, peas, jicama, celery, green onions, and sweet pepper.

2 For dressing, in a screw-top jar combine vinegar, brown sugar, parsley, salt, and white pepper. Cover and shake well. Pour the dressing over corn mixture; toss to coat. Stir in mint. Cover and refrigerate for 1 to 2 hours. Makes 10 to 12 servings.

Nutrition Facts per serving: 90 cal., 0 g total fat (0 g sat. fat), 0 mg chol., 151 mg sodium, 21 g carbo., 2 g fiber, 4 g pro.
Daily Values: 10% vit. A, 34% vit. C, 1% calcium, 9% iron
Exchanges: ½ Vegetable, 1 Starch

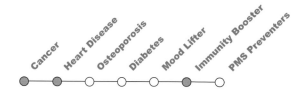

Jicama Coleslaw   **Prep:** 20 minutes   **Chill:** 2 hours

A great cabbage and apple coleslaw is made even better with sweet, nutty jicama. It adds vitamin C and potassium to the nutrient-loaded mix, making this salad a good choice to fight cancer, lower blood pressure, minimize menopausal symptoms, intensify immunity, check diabetes, and stop premenstrual syndrome.

  2 **cups shredded cabbage**

  1 **cup peeled jicama cut into bite-size strips***

  1 **medium apple, chopped, or 1 medium peach or nectarine, peeled and chopped**

  1/2 **of a small red onion, chopped (about 1/4 cup)**

  3 **tablespoons light mayonnaise dressing or salad dressing**

  2 **tablespoons snipped fresh cilantro or parsley**

  1 **tablespoon cider vinegar**

  1 1/2 **teaspoons sugar**

     Dash to 1/8 teaspoon ground red pepper

1 In a large bowl combine cabbage, jicama, apple, and red onion.

2 For dressing, in a small bowl stir together mayonnaise dressing, cilantro, vinegar, sugar, and red pepper. Pour the dressing over cabbage mixture; toss to coat. Cover and refrigerate for 2 to 4 hours. Makes 4 servings.

Nutrition Facts per serving: 91 cal., 4 g total fat (1 g sat. fat), 0 mg chol., 91 mg sodium, 14 g carbo., 2 g fiber, 1 g pro.
Daily Values: 1% vit. A, 32% vit. C, 26% calcium, 1% iron
Exchanges: 1 1/2 Vegetable, 1/2 Fruit, 1 Fat

***Note:** Store whole jicamas in the refrigerator for up to 3 weeks. If you cut them up, wrap in plastic wrap and refrigerate for up to 1 week.

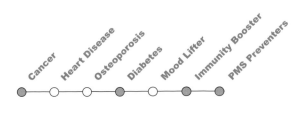

Honey-Glazed Onions

Start to Finish: 25 minutes

Honey, vinegar, and herbs turn ordinary onions into a sweet and savory side dish. Onions, containing allium, quercetin, and kaempferol, fight cancer and act as a natural antibiotic.

- **2 cups fresh or frozen small whole onions**
- **2 tablespoons honey**
- **2 tablespoons white wine vinegar**
- **1 tablespoon snipped fresh basil or 1 teaspoon dried basil, crushed**
- **¼ teaspoon ground sage**

1 If using fresh onions, in a medium covered saucepan cook onions in a small amount of boiling water for 8 to 10 minutes or just until tender; drain in colander. Cool slightly; peel. (Or cook frozen onions according to package directions; drain in colander.)

2 In the same saucepan combine honey, vinegar, basil, and sage. Add onions. Cook and stir until onions are glazed and heated through. Makes 4 servings.

Nutrition Facts per serving: 78 cal., 0 g total fat (0 g sat. fat), 0 mg chol., 4 mg sodium, 19 g carbo., 2 g fiber, 1 g pro.
Daily Values: 8% vit. C, 2% calcium, 2% iron
Exchanges: 3 Vegetable

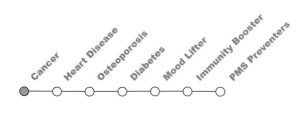

Grilled Sweet Potatoes   **Prep:** 25 minutes   **Grill:** 8 minutes

These honey-buttered potatoes should be at the top of your list for cancer-fighting antioxidants. They contain generous amounts of beta-carotene, vitamin C, and vitamin E—great for preventing cancer, heart disease, and cataracts.

2   **large sweet potatoes, halved lengthwise**

    Nonstick cooking spray

¼   **cup frozen pineapple-orange juice concentrate, thawed**

1   **tablespoon snipped fresh parsley**

1   **tablespoon margarine or butter, melted**

1   **tablespoon honey**

1   **teaspoon grated fresh ginger or ¼ teaspoon ground ginger**

1 In a medium saucepan cook potatoes in enough boiling water to cover about 15 minutes or until nearly tender; drain. Rinse with cold water; drain again. Pat dry with paper towels. Lightly coat with cooking spray.

2 Meanwhile, for glaze, in a small bowl stir together juice concentrate, parsley, margarine, honey, and ginger.

3 Grill potatoes on the rack of an uncovered grill directly over medium coals for 8 to 10 minutes or until potatoes are tender, turning once and brushing occasionally with glaze the last 5 minutes of grilling. Makes 4 servings.

Nutrition Facts per serving: 252 cal., 4 g total fat (1 g sat. fat), 1 mg chol., 58 mg sodium, 53 g carbo., 5 g fiber, 3 g pro.
Daily Values: 618% vit. A, 94% vit. C, 4% calcium, 6% iron
Exchanges: ½ Fruit, 3 Starch

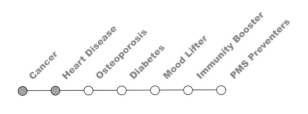

Asian Cabbage Salad, page 162

Flaxseed Rolls, page 163

161

Asian Cabbage Salad

Start to Finish: 25 minutes

Young, fresh pea pods help stabilize blood sugar, reduce heart disease, and lower cholesterol while adding color and crunch to this zestfully spiced salad. (Pictured on page 160.)

1 **cup pea pods**

3 **cups shredded Chinese cabbage or green cabbage**

1 **cup shredded radicchio or red cabbage**

1 **8³/₄-ounce can whole baby corn, rinsed, drained, and halved lengthwise**

¹/₂ **cup sliced red radishes and/or daikon**

¹/₃ **cup thinly sliced red onion**

2 **to 3 tablespoons chopped pickled ginger or 1 to 1¹/₂ teaspoons grated fresh ginger**

¹/₂ **cup fresh enoki mushrooms (optional)**

1 **recipe Asian Dressing**

1 In a small saucepan cook pea pods in a small amount of boiling water for 1 minute; drain. Cool slightly.

2 In a large salad bowl toss together pea pods, cabbage, radicchio, baby corn, red radishes, red onion, and ginger. If desired, top with enoki mushrooms and garnish with additional red radishes.

3 Shake Asian Dressing. Drizzle the dressing over salad; toss gently to coat. Makes 6 servings.

Asian Dressing: In a screw-top jar combine ¹/₄ cup rice vinegar, 2 tablespoons salad oil, 1¹/₂ teaspoons chili oil, and 1 teaspoon sugar. Cover and shake well.

Nutrition Facts per serving: 86 cal., 6 g total fat (1 g sat. fat), 0 mg chol., 20 mg sodium, 8 g carbo., 2 g fiber, 2 g pro.
Daily Values: 76% vit. C, 4% calcium, 7% iron
Exchanges: 1¹/₂ Vegetable, 1 Fat

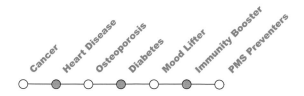

Flaxseed Rolls

Prep: 20 minutes   **Rise:** 30 minutes   **Bake:** 20 minutes

Adding flaxseeds to an easily prepared hot-roll mix creates tasty dinner rolls with a mild, nutty flavor. Rich in nutrients, flaxseeds boost the immune system, lessen the effects of menopause, and help head off cancer and heart disease. (Pictured on page 161.)

Nonstick cooking spray

2   **tablespoons flaxseeds, toasted**

1   **16-ounce package hot roll mix**

2   **teaspoons milk**

1   **teaspoon flaxseeds, crushed**

1 Coat a 13×9×2-inch baking pan with cooking spray; set aside. Place the 2 tablespoons flaxseeds in a blender container. Cover and blend until seeds are ground. (Or use a pepper mill to grind seeds.)

2 Prepare hot roll mix according to package directions, except stir in ground flaxseeds with the yeast. Shape dough into 12 smooth balls. Place the balls in the prepared baking pan. Cover and let rise in a warm place until nearly double in size (about 30 minutes).

3 Brush tops of rolls with milk; sprinkle with the 1 teaspoon flaxseeds. Bake in a 375° oven about 20 minutes or until golden brown. Remove from pan. Serve warm or cool. Makes 12 rolls.

Nutrition Facts per serving: 172 cal., 3 g total fat (0 g sat. fat), 17 mg chol., 248 mg sodium, 30 g carbo., 1 g fiber, 6 g pro.
Daily Values: 1% calcium, 6% iron
Exchanges: 2 Starch

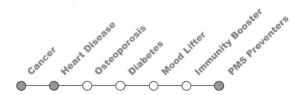

Fennel Batter Rolls

Prep: 20 minutes **Rise:** 50 minutes **Bake:** 18 minutes

These yeast rolls do not require kneading, which makes them more convenient to make. Savory onion, aromatic fennel, and pungent pepper make them the perfect accompaniment for winter soups or stews. Adding wheat germ lends a nutty flavor, and it protects against heart disease and improves the skin.

Nonstick cooking spray	2 teaspoons fennel seeds, crushed
2 cups all-purpose flour	1 teaspoon dried minced onion
1 package active dry yeast	1/2 teaspoon salt
1/2 cup cream-style cottage cheese	1/4 teaspoon coarsely ground black pepper
1/2 cup water	1 egg
1 tablespoon sugar	1/2 cup toasted wheat germ
1 tablespoon margarine or butter	

1 Lightly coat twelve 2½-inch muffin cups with cooking spray; set aside. In a medium mixing bowl stir together 1 cup of the flour and the yeast.

2 In a small saucepan heat and stir cottage cheese, water, sugar, margarine, fennel seeds, onion, salt, and black pepper just until warm (120° to 130°) and margarine almost melts. Add cottage cheese mixture to flour mixture; add egg. Beat with an electric mixer on low to medium speed for 30 seconds, scraping the sides of the bowl constantly. Beat on high speed for 3 minutes. Using a wooden spoon, stir in wheat germ and the remaining 1 cup flour (batter will be stiff).

3 Spoon the batter into the prepared muffin cups. Cover and let rise in a warm place until nearly double in size (50 to 60 minutes).

4 Bake in a 375° oven for 18 to 20 minutes or until golden brown. Immediately remove from muffin cups. Serve warm or cool. Makes 12 rolls.

Nutrition Facts per serving: 119 cal., 3 g total fat (1 g sat. fat), 19 mg chol., 150 mg sodium, 19 g carbo., 1 g fiber, 5 g pro.
Daily Values: 2% vit. A, 1% vit. C, 2% calcium, 8% iron
Exchanges: 1 Starch, ½ Fat

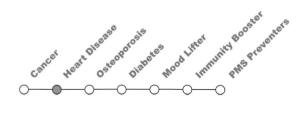

Brown Rice Pilaf

Prep: 10 minutes   **Cook:** 12 minutes   **Stand:** 5 minutes

Green onions and marjoram complement nutty brown rice, making this pilaf a perfect side dish for grilled or broiled meats, fish, or poultry. Whole-grain brown rice provides fiber to reduce the risk of cancer and help boost the immune system.

- **1   cup water**
- **1   teaspoon instant chicken bouillon granules**
- **1   cup sliced fresh mushrooms**
- **³⁄₄ cup instant brown rice**
- **¹⁄₂ cup shredded carrot**
- **³⁄₄ teaspoon snipped fresh marjoram or ¹⁄₄ teaspoon dried marjoram, crushed**
- **Dash black pepper**
- **¹⁄₄ cup thinly sliced green onions**
- **1   tablespoon snipped fresh parsley**

1 In a medium saucepan stir together water and bouillon granules. Bring to boiling. Stir in mushrooms, uncooked rice, carrot, marjoram, and black pepper. Return to boiling; reduce heat. Simmer, covered, for 12 minutes.

2 Remove saucepan from heat. Let stand, covered, for 5 minutes. Add the green onions and parsley; toss gently with a fork. Makes 4 servings.

Nutrition Facts per serving: 60 cal., 1 g total fat (0 g sat. fat), 0 mg chol., 230 mg sodium, 13 g carbo., 2 g fiber, 2 g pro.
Daily Values: 418% vit. A, 3% vit. C, 10% calcium, 1% iron
Exchanges: ¹⁄₂ Vegetable, ¹⁄₂ Starch

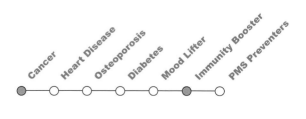

DessertsSnacks

Orange Angel Food Cake with Comote, page 168

Orange Angel Food Cake With Compote

Prep: 50 minutes **Bake:** 40 minutes **Cool:** 2 hours

The orange peel in this airy cake provides limonene, which early research suggests is a powerful anticancer agent. The dried-fruit compote also provides anticancer effects with beta-carotene and fiber. (Pictured on page 167.)

1½	cups egg whites (10 to 12 large)	1	cup dried cranberries
1	teaspoon cream of tartar	⅔	cup orange juice
1⅓	cups extra-fine granulated sugar	⅓	cup granulated sugar
1	tablespoon finely shredded orange peel	2	inches stick cinnamon
1	cup sifted cake flour	½	teaspoon vanilla
1⅓	cups water	¼	teaspoon almond extract
2	6- or 7-ounce packages dried apricots, halved		

1 In an extra-large mixing bowl let egg whites to stand at room temperature for 30 minutes. Add cream of tartar to egg whites. Beat with an electric mixer on medium speed until soft peaks form (tips curl). Gradually add the 1⅓ cups extra-fine sugar, about 2 tablespoons at a time, beating until stiff peaks form (tips stand straight).

2 Sprinkle orange peel over beaten egg whites. Sift about one-fourth of the flour over beaten egg whites; fold in gently. Repeat, folding in the remaining flour by fourths. Pour batter into an ungreased 10-inch tube pan. Gently cut through batter to remove any large air pockets.

3 Bake on the lowest rack in a 350° oven about 40 minutes or until top springs back when lightly touched. Immediately invert cake (leave in pan); cool thoroughly (about 2 hours). Loosen sides of cake from pan; remove cake.

4 Meanwhile, for compote, in a medium saucepan combine water, apricots, cranberries, orange juice, the ⅓ cup granulated sugar, the cinnamon, vanilla, and almond extract. Bring to boiling; reduce heat. Simmer, covered, for 10 minutes. Remove from heat. Discard cinnamon. Transfer the compote to a serving bowl. Serve warm or cool over cake slices. Makes 12 servings.

Nutrition Facts per serving: 257 cal., 0 g total fat (0 g sat. fat), 0 mg chol., 56 mg sodium, 61 g carbo., 3 g fiber, 5 g pro.
Daily Values: 42% vit. A, 14% vit. C, 2% calcium, 12% iron
Exchanges: 2 Fruit, 2 Starch

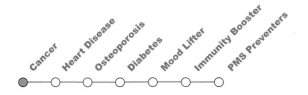

Sweet Potato Bread Pudding

Prep: 15 minutes   **Bake:** 30 minutes

Don't save sweet potatoes for Thanksgiving. They're too tasty, and you'll miss out on the beta-carotene and vitamin E they provide. Using a whole-grain bread for this recipe helps fight heart disease and cancer.

- 2 **eggs**
- 2 **egg whites**
- 1 **cup fat-free or light milk, or vanilla-flavored soy milk**
- 1 **cup mashed cooked sweet potato***
- ¼ **cup packed brown sugar**
- 1 **teaspoon ground cinnamon**
- ⅛ **teaspoon ground nutmeg**
- 3 **oups dry whole-grain bread cubes (4 slices)****
- ⅓ **cup golden raisins or snipped dried apricots**
- ¼ **cup chopped pecans, toasted**

1 In a medium bowl beat together whole eggs, egg whites, and milk. Whisk in the sweet potato, brown sugar, cinnamon, and nutmeg.

2 In a 2-quart square baking dish combine bread cubes, raisins, and pecans. Pour the egg mixture over bread mixture. Lightly press with the back of a spoon to thoroughly moisten bread.

3 Bake in a 325° oven for 30 to 35 minutes or until a knife inserted near center comes out clean. Serve warm. Makes 6 servings.

Nutrition Facts per serving: 283 cal., 7 g total fat (1 g sat. fat), 72 mg chol., 179 mg sodium, 48 g carbo., 4 g fiber, 9 g pro.
Daily Values: 192% vit. A, 17% vit. C, 10% calcium, 12% iron
Exchanges: ½ Fruit, 2½ Starch, ½ Medium Fat Meat

---

*Note: For 1 cup mashed cooked sweet potato, peel and quarter one 11- to 12-ounce sweet potato. In a small covered saucepan cook in enough boiling water to cover about 25 minutes or until tender; drain and mash.

**Note: To dry bread cubes, spread in a single layer in a 15×10×1-inch baking pan. Bake in a 300° oven for 10 to 15 minutes or until dry, stirring twice; cool. (Bread will continue to dry and crisp as it cools.) Or let stand, loosely covered, at room temperature for 8 to 12 hours.

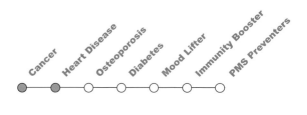

Green Tea And Tangerine Sorbet   **Prep:** 35 minutes   **Freeze:** 6 hours

Citrus flavors mingle with hints of green tea in this refreshing sorbet. Vitamin C from the tangerine juice fights cancer, protects against heart disease, helps control diabetes, increases immunity, decreases menopausal symptoms, and reduces arthritis problems. Phenolic compounds from the green tea help neutralize cancer-causing free radicals.

    1   **stalk lemongrass, cut up**
  ³⁄₄   **cup cold water**
    1   **teaspoon green tea leaves or 1 green tea bag**
    2   **cups tangerine juice**
  ¹⁄₄   **cup light-colored corn syrup**
        Tangerine cups (optional)
        Tangerine slices (optional)

1 Use the flat side of a meat mallet to slightly crush lemongrass. Place in a small saucepan; add cold water. Bring just to boiling over medium heat. Remove from heat. Add tea leaves to hot liquid. Steep for 2 minutes.

2 Strain the hot liquid into a medium bowl; discard solids. Set liquid aside to cool.

3 Stir tangerine juice and corn syrup into liquid. Pour into a nonmetal freezer container.* Cover and freeze about 4 hours or until nearly firm.

4 Break the mixture into chunks. Transfer to a chilled medium bowl. Beat with an electric mixer on medium speed until smooth. Return to freezer container. Cover and freeze about 2 hours or until firm.

5 To serve, scoop into tangerine cups (if desired) or chilled serving dishes. If desired, garnish with tangerine slices.
Makes 6 servings.

Nutrition Facts per serving: 73 cal., 0 g total fat (0 g sat. fat), 0 mg chol., 18 mg sodium, 19 g carbo., 0 g fiber, 0 g pro.
Daily Values: 7% vit. A, 43% vit. C, 2% calcium, 1% iron
Exchanges: 1 Fruit

*Note: If you like, freeze the mixture in a no-ice, no-salt, electric ice cream maker according to the manufacturer's directions.

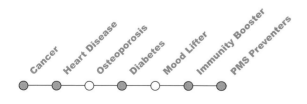

Peach Mousse

Prep: 20 minutes **Freeze:** 4 hours **Stand:** 15 minutes

This light, fruity dessert is chock-full of beta-carotene and vitamin C. The lemon peel adds intense flavor and the cancer-preventive phytochemical limonene.

 4 cups sliced, peeled fresh peaches or one 16-ounce package frozen
   unsweetened peach slices, thawed

 1/3 cup sugar

 2 teaspoons finely shredded lemon peel

 3 tablespoons lemon juice

 1/2 of an 8-ounce container frozen fat-free whipped dessert topping, thawed

 1/2 cup light dairy sour cream

1 In a large food processor bowl combine peaches, sugar, lemon peel, and lemon juice. Cover and process until mixture is smooth. Transfer to a large bowl. Fold in whipped topping and sour cream.

2 Transfer to a freezer container. Cover and freeze for 4 to 24 hours. Before serving, let stand at room temperature for 15 to 20 minutes to soften slightly. Makes 6 servings.

Nutrition Facts per serving: 200 cal., 2 g total fat (1 g sat. fat), 7 mg chol., 24 mg sodium, 44 g carbo., 5 g fiber, 3 g pro.
Daily Values: 27% vit. A, 32% vit. C, 5% calcium, 1% iron
Exchanges: 3 Fruit, 1/2 Fat

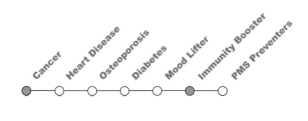

Chilly Peach Soup

Prep: 15 minutes   **Chill:** 2 hours

Whether served for dessert or a between-meal snack, this honey-sweetened, refreshing soup is loaded with summer peaches and strawberries—a great combination for fighting cancer, heart disease, and diabetes. It also increases immunity, lessens the effects of menopause, and soothes arthritis.

- **3 cups sliced, peeled fresh peaches or frozen unsweetened peach slices, thawed**
- **¹/₂ cup reduced-fat milk**
- **1 8-ounce carton vanilla low-fat yogurt**
- **3 tablespoons honey**
- **Dash ground nutmeg**
- **1 cup sliced strawberries**

1 In a large food processor bowl combine peaches and milk. Cover and process until mixture is smooth. Add yogurt, honey, and nutmeg. Cover and process until combined.

2 Transfer to a medium bowl. Cover and refrigerate for 2 to 24 hours. Before serving, stir in strawberries. Makes 4 to 6 servings.

Nutrition Facts per serving: 179 cal., 1 g total fat (1 g sat. fat), 5 mg chol., 54 mg sodium, 40 g carbo., 3 g fiber, 5 g pro.
Daily Values: 59% vit. A, 354% vit. C, 14% calcium, 4% iron
Exchanges: ¹/₂ Milk, 2 Fruit

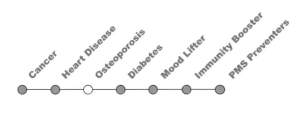

Mocha Meringue Kisses, page 176

Pineapple-Pear Crisp, page 177

Mocha Meringue Kisses

Prep: 25 minutes   **Bake:** 1 hour

These light-as-air sweet kisses are fat-free and guilt-free at just 32 calories each. The cocoa and espresso powders provide phenolic compounds, which function as antioxidants. (Pictured on page 174.)

1/3   **cup sifted powdered sugar**

2   **tablespoons unsweetened cocoa powder**

1   **tablespoon cornstarch**

1   **teaspoon instant espresso coffee powder**

3   **egg whites**

1/2   **teaspoon vanilla**

1/4   **cup granulated sugar**

1/3   **cup semisweet chocolate pieces**

1   **teaspoon shortening**

1 Line a cookie sheet with parchment paper or foil; set aside. In a small bowl stir together powdered sugar, cocoa powder, cornstarch, and espresso coffee powder; set aside.

2 In a medium mixing bowl beat egg whites and vanilla with an electric mixer on high speed until foamy. Gradually add the granulated sugar, 1 tablespoon at a time, beating until stiff peaks form (tips stand straight). Gradually fold in the cocoa mixture.

3 Transfer the mixture to a pastry bag. Pipe twenty-four 2-inch "kisses" onto the prepared cookie sheet. (Or drop mixture by rounded teaspoons onto the prepared cookie sheet.) Bake in a 250° oven for 1 hour. Cool on the cookie sheet. Remove from parchment paper.

4 In a small saucepan combine chocolate pieces and shortening. Cook and stir over low heat until chocolate pieces are melted. Drizzle the melted chocolate over cookies. Makes 24 cookies.

Nutrition Facts per cookie: 32 cal., 1 g total fat (0 g sat. fat), 0 mg chol., 7 mg sodium, 5 g carbo., 0 g fiber, 1 g pro.
Daily Values: 1% calcium
Exchanges: 1/2 Starch

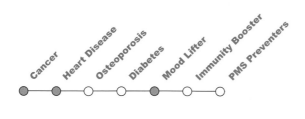

Pineapple-Pear Crisp

Prep: 20 minutes   **Bake:** 35 minutes

Fruit crisps are delicious ways to boost your fruit intake. Diets rich in fruits (and vegetables) may reduce the risk of heart disease and some types of cancer. (Pictured on page 175.)

5 **ripe pears, peeled, cored, and halved lengthwise**	$^1/_3$ **cup chopped hazelnuts, toasted**
$^1/_4$ **teaspoon ground cinnamon**	2 **tablespoons brown sugar**
3 **cups coarsely chopped pineapple**	1 **teaspoon grated fresh ginger or** $^1/_4$ **teaspoon ground ginger**
$^1/_4$ **cup honey**	$^1/_4$ **teaspoon ground nutmeg**
1 **cup rolled oats**	3 **tablespoons cooking oil**
$^1/_3$ **cup whole wheat flour**	**Low-fat vanilla frozen yogurt or ice cream (optional)**

1 Arrange pear halves, cut sides up, in a 2-quart rectangular baking dish. Sprinkle with cinnamon. Top with pineapple and drizzle with 2 tablespoons of the honey.

2 In a medium bowl combine oats, flour, hazelnuts, brown sugar, ginger, and nutmeg. Stir in the remaining 2 tablespoons honey and the oil. Sprinkle the oat mixture over fruit.

3 Bake, uncovered, in a 375° oven about 35 minutes or until pears are tender, covering with foil the last 5 minutes to prevent overbrowning. If desired, serve with frozen yogurt. Makes 10 servings.

Nutrition Facts per serving: 322 cal., 11 g total fat (3 g sat. fat), 15 mg chol., 87 mg sodium, 55 g carbo., 4 g fiber, 7 g pro.
Daily Values: 1% vit. A, 18% vit. C, 11% calcium, 7% iron
Exchanges: 2 Fruit, 1½ Starch, 2 Fat

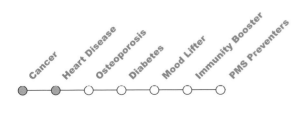

Marinated Strawberries With Frozen Yogurt

Prep: 15 minutes   **Chill:** 20 minutes

Ripe, red strawberries aren't just luscious, they're also cancer-fighters thanks to the fiber, vitamin C, and ellagic acid they contain. Choose a yogurt that states "live cultures" or "active cultures" on the label.

4   **cups (2 pints) strawberries**

2   **tablespoons sugar**

2   **tablespoons aged balsamic vinegar**

2   **tablespoons finely shredded fresh mint**

1   **tablespoon lemon juice**

3   **cups low-fat or fat-free vanilla frozen yogurt**

1 Remove stems from strawberries; halve or, if large, quarter berries lengthwise. In a medium bowl combine strawberries, sugar, balsamic vinegar, mint, and lemon juice. Cover and refrigerate at least 20 minutes or up to 4 hours.

2 To serve, spoon the strawberry mixture over scoops of frozen yogurt. Makes 6 servings.

Nutrition Facts per serving: 157 cal., 3 g total fat (2 g sat. fat), 15 mg chol., 86 mg sodium, 30 g carbo., 2 g fiber, 5 g pro.
Daily Values: 89% vit. C, 9% calcium, 4% iron
Exchanges: 1 Fruit, 1 Starch

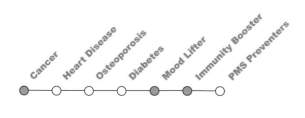

Strawberry-Mango Soy Milk Smoothie   **Start to Finish:** 10 minutes

Vanilla soy milk forms the base for this fruity smoothie. Plain soy milk has a nutty flavor and can substitute for regular milk in recipes. Both flavored and unflavored soy milk provide soy protein, which helps reduce blood cholesterol levels.

1	cup vanilla-flavored soy milk
¼	cup orange juice
¼	cup refrigerated or frozen egg product, thawed
1	to 2 tablespoons honey
½	cup chopped mango
½	cup frozen strawberries, raspberries, blueberries, or boysenberries

1 In a blender container combine soy milk, orange juice, egg product, and honey. Cover and blend for 10 seconds.

2 Add mango and frozen desired berries. Cover and blend until mixture is smooth. Immediately pour into 2 tall glasses. Makes 2 servings.

Nutrition Facts per serving: 138 cal., 3 g total fat (0 g sat. fat), 0 mg chol., 66 mg sodium, 24 g carbo., 3 g fiber, 7 g pro.
Daily Values: 36% vit. A, 79% vit. C, 3% calcium, 9% iron
Exchanges: ½ Milk, 1 Fruit, ½ Very Lean Meat

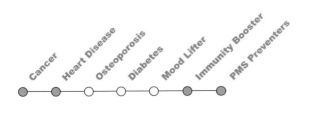

Fruited Yogurt Brûlée

Prep: 20 minutes **Bake:** 7 minutes

A quick bake makes a crisp brown sugar crust on these low-fat, fruit-filled desserts. The ricotta cheese and yogurt contribute calcium to strengthen bones and reduce heart disease. The fresh fruits offer fiber and vitamin C to battle cancer, fight heart disease, and reduce symptoms of menopause.

   6   cups fresh fruit (such as blueberries and/or sliced strawberries,

   bananas, mangoes, papayas, apricots, pears, peaches, or pineapple)

   1   8-ounce carton lowfat vanilla yogurt

   ½   cup part-skim ricotta cheese

   ¼   cup packed brown sugar

1 Divide fruit among four 12- to 16-ounce au gratin dishes. Place dishes in a 15×10×1-inch baking pan. In a small bowl stir together yogurt and ricotta cheese. Spoon the yogurt mixture over fruit. Sprinkle with brown sugar.

2 Bake, uncovered, in a 450° oven for 7 to 8 minutes or until brown sugar is melted. Serve immediately. Makes 4 servings.

Nutrition Facts per serving: 211 cal., 4 g total fat (2 g sat. fat), 13 mg chol., 86 mg sodium, 39 g carbo., 5 g fiber, 7 g pro.
Daily Values: 5% vit. A, 205% vit. C, 23% calcium, 7% iron
Exchanges: ½ Milk, 2 Fruit

Cancer　Heart Disease　Osteoporosis　Diabetes　Mood Lifter　Immunity Booster　PMS Preventers

Apricot Granola Bars

Prep: 15 minutes   **Bake:** 20 minutes

Toasted wheat germ teams up with whole wheat flour, rolled oats, almonds, and sesame seeds to provide a walloping serving of whole grains and nuts—great for lowering cholesterol, improving skin, and reducing the chance of cancer. Dried apricots add a tangy sweetness and lend potassium, which helps regulate blood pressure.

	Nonstick cooking spray	2	tablespoons sesame seeds
2	cups quick-cooking rolled oats	¹/₂	teaspoon ground cinnamon
1	cup sliced almonds	¹/₈	teaspoon salt
1	cup finely snipped dried apricots	2	beaten eggs
¹/₃	cup toasted wheat germ	¹/₂	cup honey
¹/₄	cup whole wheat flour	¹/₃	cup cooking oil
¹/₄	cup packed brown sugar	1	teaspoon vanilla

1 Line a 13×9×2-inch baking pan with foil. Lightly coat the foil with cooking spray; set aside.

2 In a large bowl stir together oats, almonds, apricots, wheat germ, flour, brown sugar, sesame seeds, cinnamon, and salt. In a small bowl combine eggs, honey, oil, and vanilla. Add the egg mixture to oat mixture; stir until moistened.

3 Press the mixture firmly and evenly into the prepared baking pan. Bake in a 325° oven for 20 to 25 minutes or until edges are lightly browned. Cool in pan on a wire rack. Use the foil to lift cookies from pan. Cut into bars. Makes 24 bars.

Nutrition Facts per serving: 154 cal., 7 g total fat (1 g sat. fat), 18 mg chol., 20 mg sodium, 20 g carbo., 2 g fiber, 4 g pro.
Daily Values: 8% vit. A, 3% calcium, 6% iron
Exchanges: ¹/₂ Fruit, 1 Starch, 1 Fat

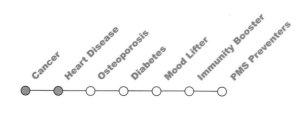

Carrot Hummus

Prep: 15 minutes   **Chill:** 1 hour

Carrots add more than color and sweetness to this spicy hummus. Their abundance of beta-carotene, combined with the health attributes of garbanzo beans, makes this dip a great choice to boost immunity, fight cancer, alleviate arthritis, enhance the skin, control blood sugar, and increase energy.

1   **cup chopped carrots**

1   **15-ounce can garbanzo beans, rinsed and drained**

¼   **cup tahini (sesame seed paste)**

2   **tablespoons lemon juice**

2   **cloves garlic, quartered**

½   **teaspoon ground cumin**

¼   **teaspoon salt**

2   **tablespoons snipped fresh parsley**

    Assorted dippers (such as toasted whole wheat pita bread

      triangles, vegetable sticks, and/or whole-grain crackers)

1 In a small covered saucepan cook carrots in a small amount of boiling water for 6 to 8 minutes or until tender; drain. In a food processor bowl combine cooked carrots, garbanzo beans, tahini, lemon juice, garlic, cumin, and salt. Cover and process until mixture is smooth. Transfer to a small serving bowl. Stir in parsley.

2 Cover and refrigerate at least 1 hour or up to 3 days. If necessary, stir in enough water, 1 tablespoon at a time, to make of dipping consistency. Serve with assorted dippers. Makes sixteen 2-tablespoon servings.

Nutrition Facts per serving: 60 cal., 2 g total fat (0 g sat. fat), 0 mg chol., 124 mg sodium, 8 g carbo., 2 g fiber, 2 g pro.
Daily Values: 49% vit. A, 5% vit. C, 2% calcium, 3% iron
Exchanges: ½ Starch, ½ Fat

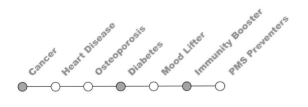

Veggie Tempura With Honey-Mustard Sauce

Prep: 30 minutes **Bake:** 9 minutes

The wide variety of veggies in this tempura provides vitamins, minerals, and health-promoting plant compounds. A snack like this one is good choice because of the high amount of fiber it provides. A diet high in fiber is beneficial in staving off cancer and heart disease and also helps keep blood sugars in check.

Nonstick cooking spray

1½ cups panko crumbs (Japanese-style bread crumbs)

¼ teaspoon salt

1½ cups cauliflower florets

1½ cups small fresh mushrooms, stems removed

1 medium sweet potato, peeled and cut into
    3×½-inch strips

1 small zucchini, sliced ¼ inch thick

1 small red onion, sliced ½ inch thick and
    separated into rings

1 cup green beans

1 cup sugar snap peas

¼ cup all-purpose flour

2 slightly beaten eggs

2 tablespoons margarine or butter, melted

1 recipe Honey-Mustard Sauce

1 Coat a 15×10×1-inch baking pan with cooking spray; set aside. In a medium bowl combine panko crumbs and salt. In a large bowl toss the vegetables in flour, shaking to remove any excess flour. Dip the vegetables, a few at a time, into the eggs, then into the panko crumb mixture to coat.

2 Place the vegetables in a single layer in the prepared baking pan. (Vegetables may be prepared ahead. Cover and refrigerate for up to 3 hours.) Drizzle the vegetables with melted margarine.

3 Bake, uncovered, in a 450° oven for 9 to 11 minutes or until vegetables are golden brown, gently stirring twice. Serve immediately with Honey-Mustard Sauce. Makes 6 servings.

Honey-Mustard Sauce: In a small bowl stir together 1 cup Dijon-style mustard and 2 tablespoons honey.

Nutrition Facts per serving: 257 cal., 10 g total fat (3 g sat. fat), 83 mg chol., 443 mg sodium, 35 g carbo., 4 g fiber, 10 g pro.
Daily Values: 8% vit. A, 32% vit. C, 9% calcium, 13% iron
Exchanges: 1 Vegetable, 2 Starch, 1½ Fat

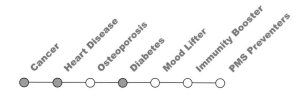

Spiced Popcorn

Start to Finish: 10 minutes

Popcorn is more than a crunchy low-cal snack. It's a good source of insoluble fiber, which promotes a healthy digestive system. Popcorn is also a whole-grain food that protects against heart disease and some types of cancer.

- ½ **teaspoon ground cumin**
- ½ **teaspoon chili powder**
- ¼ **to ½ teaspoon salt**
- **Dash ground red pepper**
- **Dash ground cinnamon**
- 12 **cups popped popcorn**
- **Nonstick cooking spray**

1 In a small bowl stir together cumin, chili powder, salt, red pepper, and cinnamon.

2 Spread popped popcorn in an even layer in a large shallow baking pan. Lightly coat popcorn with cooking spray. Sprinkle the cumin mixture evenly over popcorn; toss to coat. Makes twelve 1-cup servings.

Nutrition Facts per serving: 31 cal., 0 g total fat (0 g sat. fat), 0 mg chol., 50 mg sodium, 6 g carbo., 1 g fiber, 1 g pro.
Daily Values: 1% vit. A, 1% iron
Exchanges: ½ Starch

Indian Spiced Popcorn: Prepare Spiced Popcorn as directed, except substitute ½ teaspoon curry powder, ½ teaspoon garam masala, ¼ teaspoon ground turmeric, and ¼ teaspoon black pepper for the cumin, chili powder, ground red pepper, and cinnamon.

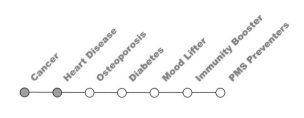

Herbed Soy Nuts And Seeds   **Prep:** 10 minutes   **Bake:** 15 minutes

This addictive party mix is a tasty way to add soy to your diet. Research shows that consuming at least 25 grams of soy protein daily may reduce the risk of heart disease. Soy has also been shown to reduce menopausal symptoms. A one-quarter cup serving of this mix provides 4 grams of soy protein.

1	tablespoon olive oil or cooking oil
1	teaspoon chili powder
1	teaspoon dried basil, crushed
$\frac{1}{2}$	teaspoon dried oregano, crushed
$\frac{1}{4}$	teaspoon garlic powder
$1\frac{1}{2}$	cups salted roasted soy nuts*
$\frac{1}{2}$	cup raw pumpkin seeds
$\frac{1}{2}$	cup dried vegetables (such as carrots, corn, and/or peas)

1 In a medium bowl stir together oil, chili powder, basil, oregano, and garlic powder. Add soy nuts and pumpkin seeds; toss to coat. Spread the mixture in a 13×9×2-inch baking pan.

2 Bake, uncovered, in a 350° oven for 15 to 20 minutes or until soy nuts are toasted, stirring after 10 minutes. Stir in dried vegetables. Makes 10 servings.

Nutrition Facts per serving: 126 cal., 8 g total fat (2 g sat. fat), 0 mg chol., 48 mg sodium, 8 g carbo., 2 g fiber, 7 g pro.
Daily Values: 127% vit. A, 4% vit. C, 4% calcium, 11% iron
Exchanges: $\frac{1}{2}$ Starch, 1 Very Lean Meat, 1 Fat

---

*Note: If using unsalted roasted soy nuts, add $\frac{1}{8}$ teaspoon salt to the chili powder mixture.

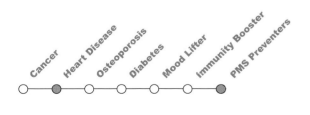

Index

Metric

Metric Cooking Hints

By making a few conversions, cooks in Australia, Canada, and the United Kingdom can use the recipes in this book with confidence. The charts on this page provide a guide for converting measurements from the U.S. customary system, which is used throughout this book, to the imperial and metric systems. There also is a conversion table for oven temperatures to accommodate the differences in oven calibrations.

Product Differences: Most of the ingredients called for in the recipes in this book are available in English-speaking countries. However, some are known by different names. Here are some common U.S. American ingredients and their possible counterparts:

- Sugar is granulated or castor sugar.
- Powdered sugar is icing sugar.
- All-purpose flour is plain household flour or white flour. When self-rising flour is used in place of all-purpose flour in a recipe that calls for leavening, omit the leavening agent (baking soda or baking powder) and salt.
- Light-colored corn syrup is golden syrup.
- Cornstarch is cornflour.
- Baking soda is bicarbonate of soda.
- Vanilla is vanilla essence.
- Green, red, or yellow sweet peppers are capsicums.
- Golden raisins are sultanas.

Volume and Weight: U.S. Americans traditionally use cup measures for liquid and solid ingredients. The chart, below, shows the approximate imperial and metric equivalents. If you are accustomed to weighing solid ingredients, the following approximate equivalents will help.

- 1 cup butter, castor sugar, or rice = 8 ounces = about 230 grams
- 1 cup flour = 4 ounces = about 115 grams
- 1 cup icing sugar = 5 ounces = about 140 grams

Spoon measures are used for smaller amounts of ingredients. Although the size of the tablespoon varies slightly in different countries, for practical purposes and for recipes in this book, a straight substitution is all that's necessary.

Measurements made using cups or spoons always should be level unless stated otherwise.

Equivalents: U.S. = Australia/U.K.

$\frac{1}{5}$ teaspoon = 1 ml	$\frac{1}{2}$ cup = 120 ml
$\frac{1}{4}$ teaspoon = 1.25 ml	$\frac{2}{3}$ cup = 160 ml
$\frac{1}{2}$ teaspoon = 2.5 ml	$\frac{3}{4}$ cup = 180 ml
1 teaspoon = 5 ml	1 cup = 240 ml
1 tablespoon = 15 ml	2 cups = 475 ml
1 fluid ounce = 30 ml	1 quart = 1 liter
$\frac{1}{4}$ cup = 60 ml	$\frac{1}{2}$ inch = 1.25 cm
$\frac{1}{3}$ cup = 80 ml	1 inch = 2.5 cm

Baking Pan Sizes

U.S.	Metric
8×1½-inch round baking pan	20×4-cm cake tin
9×1½-inch round baking pan	23×4-cm cake tin
11×7×1½-inch baking pan	28×18×4-cm baking tin
13×9×2-inch baking pan	32×23×5-cm baking tin
2-quart rectangular baking dish	28×18×4-cm baking tin
15×10×1-inch baking pan	38×25.5×2.5-cm baking tin (Swiss roll tin)
9-inch pie plate	22×4- or 23×4-cm pie plate
7- or 8-inch springform pan	18- or 20-cm springform or loose-bottom cake tin
9×5×3-inch loaf pan	23×13×8-cm or 2-pound narrow loaf tin or pâté tin
1½-quart casserole	1.5-liter casserole
2-quart casserole	2-liter casserole

Oven Temperature Equivalents

Fahrenheit Setting	Celsius Setting*	Gas Setting
300°F	150°C	Gas mark 2 (very low)
325°F	170°C	Gas mark 3 (low)
350°F	180°C	Gas mark 4 (moderate)
375°F	190°C	Gas mark 5 (moderately hot)
400°F	200°C	Gas mark 6 (hot)
425°F	220°C	Gas mark 7 (hot)
450°F	230°C	Gas mark 8 (very hot)
475°F	240°C	Gas mark 9 (very hot)
Broil		Grill

*Electric and gas ovens may be calibrated using Celsius. However, for an electric oven, increase the Celsius setting 10 to 20 degrees when cooking above 160°C. For convection or forced-air ovens (gas or electric), lower the temperature setting 10°C when cooking at all heat levels.